PREDICTING THE MARKETS
TOPICAL STUDY #4

S&P 500
Earnings, Valuation,
and the Pandemic

A Primer for Investors

Edward Yardeni
Joseph Abbott

YRI PRESS

Predicting the Markets Topical Study #4:
S&P 500 Earnings, Valuation, and the Pandemic: A Primer for Investors

Copyright © 2020 Edward Yardeni

ISBN: 978-1-948025-08-9 (paperback)
ISBN: 978-1-948025-09-6 (eBook)

Published by YRI Books, a division of Yardeni Research, Inc.
68 Wheatley Road, Suite 1100
Brookville, NY USA 11545

Contact us: **requests@yardeni.com**

Excerpted, updated, and expanded from *Predicting the Markets: A Professional Autobiography* (2018).

For our children

Melissa, Sarah, Samuel, David, and Laura Yardeni
&
Jessica Abbott

Think ahead and move forward.

Author's Note

This study is another in a series of Topical Studies examining issues that I discussed in my book *Predicting the Markets: A Professional Autobiography* (2018) but in greater detail and on a more current basis. Previous studies in this series, which are available on my Amazon homepage, include:

Fed Watching for Fun & Profit: A Primer for Investors (2020)

Stock Buybacks: The True Story (2019)

The Yield Curve: What Is It Really Predicting? (2019)

The charts at the end of this study were current as of September 14, 2020. Updates (in color), as well as linked endnotes and appendices are available at **www.yardenibook.com/studies**.

Institutional investors are invited to sign up for the Yardeni Research service on a complimentary trial basis at **www.yardeni.com/trial-registration**.

Contents

"In other words, the market is not a weighing machine, on which the value of each issue is recorded by an exact and impersonal mechanism, in accordance with its specific qualities. Rather should we say that the market is a voting machine, whereon countless individuals register choices which are the product partly of reason and partly of emotion."

—*Benjamin Graham,* Security Analysis *(1934)*

Introduction

I started my career on Wall Street in 1978. I spent the prior year at the Federal Reserve Bank of New York in the economics research department after receiving my undergraduate degree in economics and government from Cornell University in 1972 and my PhD in economics from Yale University in 1976. Over the past 40-plus years, I've worked as both the chief economist and the chief investment strategist at several firms on Wall Street. Since January 2007, I've been the president of my own consulting firm, Yardeni Research, Inc.

My job continues to be to predict the financial markets, particularly the major stock, bond, commodity, and foreign exchange markets around the world. I've learned a lot about these markets over the years. I recently started sharing what I've learned in a series of books and studies.

In this study, I will focus on the S&P 500 stock price index, examining how it is determined by the earnings of the 500 companies that are included in the index and the valuation of those earnings by the stock market.

Why pick the S&P 500?

The S&P 500 is a stock market index that measures the stock price performance of 500 large companies listed on stock exchanges in the United States. It is one of the most widely followed equity indexes. The stocks in this index are a representative sample of leading companies in leading industries. Many equity managers benchmark the performance of their portfolios to the S&P 500. Among the largest exchange-traded funds are those that track the S&P 500. The S&P 500 represents more than 83% of the total domestic US equity market capitalization.[1]

The widely followed Dow Jones Industrials Average (DJIA) has only 30 companies. It was launched in 1896 and was a spin-off of the Dow Jones Transportation Average, which was first compiled in 1884 by Charles Dow, the co-founder of Dow Jones & Company. The S&P 500 dates back to 1923. That year, the Standard Statistics Company (founded in 1906 as the "Standard Statistics Bureau") developed its first stock market index, consisting of the stocks of 233 US companies and 26 industries, computed weekly. (The company also began rating mortgage bonds in 1923.) In 1926, it developed a 90-stock index, computed daily. In 1941, Poor's Publishing merged with Standard Statistics Company to form Standard & Poor's (S&P). On March 4, 1957, the index was expanded to its current 500 companies and was renamed the "S&P 500 Stock Composite Index."

The components of the S&P 500 index and other S&P indexes are selected by the firm's US Index Committee, which meets monthly. All committee members are full-time professional members of the firm's Indices staff. At each meeting, committee members review pending corporate actions that may affect the indexes' constituent companies, statistics comparing the indexes' composition to the broad stock market, candidate companies under consideration for addition to an index, and the bearing of any significant market events on the indexes.

The committee identifies important industries within the US equity market, approximates the relative weight of these industries in terms of market capitalization, and then allocates a representative sample of stocks within each industry of the S&P 500. There are 11 sectors according to the Global Industry Classification Standard (GICS): Communication Services, Consumer Discretionary, Consumer Staples, Energy, Financials, Health Care, Industrials,

Information Technology, Materials, Real Estate, and Utilities.[2] These sectors are further divided into 24 industry groups, 69 industries, and 158 subindustries.

Candidates for inclusion in the S&P 500 index must meet specific criteria in eight areas: market capitalization, liquidity, domicile, public float, GICS, financial viability, length of time publicly traded, and stock exchange listing. The index is reconstituted quarterly, though changes are made infrequently.

The S&P 500 index is a free-float, capitalization-weighted index. That means that companies are weighted in the index in proportion to their market capitalizations. To determine the market-capitalization weight of a company, only the number of shares available for public trading (free float) is used. Shares held by insiders or by controlling shareholders that are not publicly traded are excluded from the calculation. The largest companies (based on market capitalization) in the S&P 500 account for a substantial portion of its total market capitalization. Since the index is market-capitalization weighted, these companies have the greatest influence on the index's price performance.

Notwithstanding occasional bear markets, the S&P 500 has been a great investment over the years—so much so that "S&P" could stand for "Success & Profit." Since January 1, 1955, through September 2, 2020, the index has been down in bear markets during 3,029 of the 16,535 trading days—i.e., just 18.3% of the time. It has risen at a compounded annual rate of 6%, a rate that doubles the value of this portfolio every 12 years. And that doesn't include the dividend return provided by many of the S&P 500 companies.

The first chapter in our study covers the various measures of earnings for the S&P 500 and why we favor forward earnings among them. The second chapter discusses various models of valuation, again focusing on the S&P 500. The final chapter uses the resulting analytical framework to review how it has worked in good times and bad, focusing on the Great Financial Crisis and the Great Virus Crisis.

Chapter 1
S&P 500 Earnings

Discounting Forward Earnings

This primer for investors develops a simple framework for analyzing and forecasting the widely followed S&P 500 stock price index (P). Doing so should be simple enough. One only needs to forecast two numbers—i.e., earnings per share (E) and the price-to-earnings valuation ratio (P/E) in the stock market equation:

$$P = P/E \times E$$

Forecasting these two variables is easy; getting them right is the hard part. Most investment strategists use their own "top-down" earnings forecasts for the current year and coming year and multiply them by their forecasts of the P/E for the current year and the next year. I modified this approach during 2001 with my "Earnings Squiggles" analytical framework. I start with the "bottom-up" earnings expectations of industry analysts, benchmarking my outlook to theirs.

Why incorporate analysts' expectations into my thinking about the prospects for earnings? The stock market discounts future expected earnings. Past and current earnings are relevant, but only to the extent that they influence the outlook for future earnings.

Whose earnings expectations does the market discount, and how far into the future?

The market doesn't discount the earnings expectations of individual investment strategists or even the consensus expectations of top-down strategists. It discounts the bottom-up consensus earnings expectations of industry analysts. It's those expectations that I want to quantify and use in the stock market equation as a benchmark for my own forecasts.

Therefore, the bottom-up earnings expectations data that I use are an aggregation of the estimates for all the stocks in the S&P 500 covered by industry analysts. As the saying goes, "the stock market is a market of stocks"—so using bottom-up earnings estimates makes more sense than using top-down forecasts. Since the stock market is forward-looking, with stock prices discounting future earnings prospects, I don't use so-called trailing earnings in the stock market equation.

More specifically, I believe that stock investors are basing their decisions on the outlook for earnings over the year ahead (i.e., the next 12 months, or 52 weeks). Experienced investors recognize that anything beyond that is too far off to forecast with any degree of accuracy. Investors obviously rely on industry analysts for their insights about earnings. Consequently, I view analysts' consensus forecasts as a treasure trove of valuable information on earnings for the stock market equation. However, analysts don't provide rolling earnings forecasts for the coming 12 months. Like company managements, they focus on quarterly estimates for the current year and the coming one.

Fortunately, I/B/E/S data by Refinitiv fills this void. I/B/E/S, which stands for "Institutional Brokers' Estimate System," compiles analysts' consensus earnings-per-share expectations for each of the S&P 500 corporations and combines them to calculate the consensus expected earnings per share of the overall S&P 500 for each of the quarters of the current year and the coming year. I/B/E/S provides a useful proxy called "12-month forward consensus expected earnings" for the S&P 500. It is a time-weighted average of the analysts' consensus earnings estimates for the current year and the coming year. This series, which starts during

September 1978, supplies the forward-looking earnings (E) and the forward-looking valuation (P/E) I need to assess the stock market.

In 2000, I hired Joe Abbott from I/B/E/S to help me develop an in-house database and analytical tools to monitor and analyze the consensus data so that we could track forward earnings for the S&P 500, its 11 sectors, and the more than 100 industries that compose them. Joe had been a senior equity strategist at I/B/E/S for 14 years, before it was acquired by Thomson Financial during 2000, so he was exceptionally well qualified for the job. Together, we developed a simple graphical framework for visualizing the I/B/E/S consensus data.

We dubbed the framework "Earnings Squiggles" because the time series for each calendar-year forecast, which we update monthly, tend to look like squiggles (*Fig. 1* and *Fig. 2*). Forward earnings is simply a time-weighted average of the analysts' latest consensus estimate of earnings for the current-year squiggle and for the coming year's squiggle. At the start of a year (i.e., in January), forward earnings is identical to the current year's consensus forecast. One month later (i.e., in February), forward earnings is the weighted average of 11/12 of the current year's estimate and 1/12 of the coming year's estimate. So as any given year progresses, forward earnings gradually converges with the estimate for the coming year, and by January it is once again identical to next year's consensus outlook. Of course, the next year's earnings estimate is a moving target because it changes as analysts revise their earnings estimates, as does the current year's estimate. (See *Appendix 1, Deriving 12-Month Forward Earnings*.)

In the monthly charts, we show every year's squiggle spanning 25 months from February to February (i.e., 11 months before a given year begins and two months after it ends). That's because for calculating forward earnings, the next year only enters the calculation once the current year is one month old, as noted above.

Then the squiggles run through the 12 months of the actual year and another two months after it ends. That's because the fourth quarter's results for each year are reported in the earnings season during January, with some stragglers during February. Each year's squiggle starts the preceding February since it needs to be time-weighted with the current year. Each year's squiggle ends during the following year's February, after earnings are released for the final quarter of the year it covers, though that last quarterly report only matters through the end of its year.

This may be a bit confusing, so a more specific example should help to make sense of it all. During January 2018, forward earnings was identical to the consensus estimate for all of 2018. No weight was given to 2019's estimate. During February 2018, we started to track the 2019 squiggle because forward earnings represented 11/12 of the latest 2018 estimate and 1/12 of the latest 2019 consensus estimate. By January 2019, the 2018 squiggle was no longer relevant, but we plotted the squiggle through February 2019 (when data for the final quarter of 2018 were available) to show that it had converged to closely match the actual result for 2018.

One of the biggest advantages of the I/B/E/S forward earnings is that the data are available much more frequently than the measures of actual profits that are provided quarterly, with a lag of a few weeks, for the S&P 500 by Standard & Poor's and for the corporate sector broadly by the US Commerce Department's Bureau of Economic Analysis (BEA) in its National Income and Product Accounts (NIPA). The Earnings Squiggles and forward earnings for the S&P 500 are available not only monthly from September 1978 but also weekly from March 1994 (*Fig. 3* and *Fig. 4*).

We have 40 years of complete annual squiggles from 1980 through 2019, with 25 months of data for each one of them. From the beginning to the end of each annual squiggle, estimates fell for 31 of those years and rose for nine of them. The squiggles tend to decline over time because analysts tend to be overly optimistic about the outlook for their companies' earnings the further in the future they are. The up-year exceptions were 1980, 1988, 1995, 2004, 2005, 2006, 2010, 2011, and 2018 (*Fig. 5*). Of course, the steepest downward slopes have occurred during recessions, when analysts are scrambling to cut their estimates. The few years when they raised their estimates in the past tended to be during economic recoveries, especially following bad recessions during which analysts had become too pessimistic. The overall average decline for the 25 months of the 40 years was –11.9%, with the 31 down years averaging –17.5% and the nine up years averaging 7.0%.

Joe and I track Net Earnings Revisions Indexes (NERIs) for the S&P 500 as well as its 11 sectors and 100-plus industries. NERIs show the percentage of analysts' forward earnings estimates that have been revised higher minus the percentage of them that have been revised lower, divided by the total number of forward earnings estimates. The resulting indexes are extremely volatile on weekly and monthly bases and tend to be most active around earnings reporting seasons, when analysts are more likely to adjust their forecasts. We've found that the three-month average of NERIs provides the most useful information, since it encompasses the entire quarterly earnings cycle. Our data start during January 1985 on a monthly basis and mid-January 2006 on a weekly basis.

In the past, the S&P 500's NERI always turned negative during recessions and tended to be positive during recoveries (*Fig. 6*). During expansions, it has shown mixed performances. Given that most Earnings Squiggles have downward slopes, NERIs tend to have a negative bias. So during expansions, we are not overly concerned to see negative NERIs and give more weight to the positive ones.

It's human nature for industry analysts to be biased toward optimism about the prospects of the companies they follow. Most have a strong professional interest in their designated industries and companies. Most prefer to give buy ratings rather than sell ratings, which is why they have more of the former than the latter. Analysts don't want to follow companies that are likely to go out of business. If they are following a dying industry, they can score points by being bearish ahead of the curve. However, eventually they'll have to start all over again covering a different industry. Also, analysts are loath to get too negative on companies that have investment banking relationships with their firm. Given analysts' inherent optimism, savvy investors know that when analysts downgrade their recommendation on a stock from "buy" to "hold," they probably mean "sell."

Now, imagine the following stylized conversation between a "sell-side" industry analyst and a "buy-side" portfolio manager:

> Jan: Jim, thanks for visiting us today and sharing your earnings outlook for your industry, especially for ABC Corp., which we own. We always value your insights and analysis. However, you're always too optimistic on earnings and invariably lower them. When might you be cutting your estimates yet again for this year?

> Jim: Jan, thanks for taking the meeting. Look, this year is half over. Let's not dwell on it too much. Let's talk about next year. It's going to be a great one for the company.

That in a nutshell is how earnings are discounted by the stock market, in our opinion, and why we are fans of forward earnings as the intuitively "correct" earnings measure to use in the stock market equation to forecast the market. The average portfolio manager is relying on the average earnings expectations of the analysts over the next 12 months. The P/E earnings valuation multiple in the stock market equation, however, is determined by investors, not analysts. It's up to investors to decide how much they are willing to pay for the time-weighted average of analysts' consensus earnings expectations for this year and next year.

We need to stress a very important point about the Earnings Squiggles and forward earnings: The stock market can go up when analysts are reducing their earnings estimates for the current year and the coming year. We are often asked how this can be. The answer is that if next year's estimate exceeds the time-weighted average, forward earnings will rise as next year gets more weight while this year gets less. Arithmetically, forward earnings converges to next year's consensus estimate. While it is possible for forward earnings to rise if the current-year consensus plunges, often next year's estimate will take a dive too. Let's continue the above conversation:

> Jan: Okay, Jim, we can talk about next year now that it's fast approaching. However, I see in your spreadsheet that you've already started lowering your estimate for next year!

> Jim: That's true, Jan, but my forecast for this year is still better than last year's result, and next year still exceeds my number for this year. Things are continuing to get better for the company, though not quite as great as I had been predicting.

Institutional investors (on the buy side) clearly value the opinions of industry analysts (on the sell side). Why else would Wall Street hire them and pay them so well? Few investors have the time or the in-house resources to do their own industry-specific research and channel checks. Those who do have their own analysts sometimes hire them from Wall Street. In-house analysts are deluged by research provided by Street analysts and often develop close professional relationships with the ones they respect the most. Indeed, many buy-side money management firms have a voting system whereby their internal analysts collectively allocate commission dollars to the sell-side firms whose analysts have helped them the most.

To assess its accuracy, the 12-month forward earnings forecast can be pushed ahead by a year and compared to actual quarterly S&P 500 operating earnings on a four-quarter-trailing basis—i.e., the moving sum over the past four quarters (*Fig. 7* and *Fig. 8*). The former turns out to be a very good leading indicator of the latter, with one rather important exception.

Collectively, industry analysts generally don't do a very good job of anticipating recessions, which causes them to slash their earnings estimates for both the current and the coming years. Conversely, during economic expansions they do a very good job of forecasting earnings over the year ahead using the forward earnings proxy. Fortunately, expansions tend to last much longer than recessions. Since 1945, there have been 12 recessions that lasted 130 months in total, just 15% of the time through the end of 2019.

Analysts aren't economists. It isn't their job to see a recession coming. Besides, investors would probably ignore such warnings coming from an analyst unless he or she had insights from a company that was especially well positioned to see a recession coming. That may happen occasionally, but there is no evidence that analysts collectively provide any early warnings of a coming recession.

Predicting recessions is what economists are supposed to do, and we don't do a very good job of it. Indeed, it seems that every recession produces a superstar economist who was alone in anticipating the latest downturn. Of course, at the end of the day, it is up to investors to anticipate recessions. Some rely on their favorite economists to assess this risk. Most simply react to the news headlines. If the economic news is bad, many will sell stocks and raise their cash position even if industry analysts remain upbeat on earnings. If the news turns good, then stocks will rebound, and the analysts' forecasts will have more credibility.

Joe and I also track analysts' consensus earnings expectations for each of the quarters of the current year and coming year on a weekly basis. That provides us with a window into an interesting tendency of the "too-high" analysts to lower their estimates as earnings seasons approach and the "low or just right" analysts to hold their forecasts steady. Often, that sets the market up for a positive earnings surprise, which looks like an upside earnings hook, when actual reported results turn out to be better than consensus estimates.

Furthermore, company managements generally deliver bad news and warnings during the "preannouncements" that precede earnings reporting seasons. The good news is typically held back by company managements, often causing their stock price to pop when they release the better-than-expected results. They will also get a bigger positive surprise score in the consensus database services. The size of the surprise is an oft-used screening criteria for investors who rely on quantitative analysis. This game causes the aggregate forecast often to fall ahead of actual results because downward revisions are dominating the analysts' community, often setting the stage for the upside hook.

Analysts' quarterly consensus earnings expectations for the S&P 500 are available on a weekly basis from late March 1994. Joe and I track them in our chart publication titled *Stock Market Briefing: S&P 500 Earnings Squiggles Annually & Quarterly*.[3] From the first quarter of 1994 through the second quarter of 2020, there were 106 quarterly squiggles. Of these, 87 ended with earnings hooks, where the actual results were better than analysts predicted at the start of the earnings season by at least 0.1%. Squiggles reflecting estimates that were beat by 3.0% or more totaled 54, while only 20 squiggles reflected big positive surprises exceeding 5.0%. The longest streak of positive surprises occurred during every quarter from the first quarter of 2009 through the second quarter of 2020.[4] Such upward surprises don't happen during recessions, when actual results often turn out to be worse than the rapidly falling estimates, so the earnings hook is much smaller or nonexistent.

Of course, most of the information in companies' quarterly earnings reports is old news, having happened during the previous quarter. However, the information does provide insights into the likely future course of a company's earnings. From the perspective of our forward earnings analytical approach, the fourth quarter of each year is the least important. That's because by the time the results are reported during January and February of the next year, the previous year (including the fourth quarter, of course) is irrelevant to forward earnings, which no longer gives any weight to it. However, each quarter's results can significantly impact earnings revisions for coming quarters. This will be an important consideration in Chapter 3, when we discuss the timing of the events that kicked off the Great Financial Crisis and the Great Virus Crisis, specifically the Lehman calamity late in 2008 and the declaration of the COVID-19 pandemic early in 2020.

Lots of S&P 500 Earnings Measures

Above we examined the relationship between forward earnings and the actual operating earnings of the S&P 500, both calculated using I/B/E/S data. The former tends to be a good leading indicator of the latter when the economy is growing but not when it is falling into a recession. There are other measures of S&P 500 profits. They aren't forward-looking or available weekly; only forward earnings has these advantages. The rest represent actual quarterly results compiled by other private-sector data vendors. What many of these series offer are more historical data than are available for forward earnings, which starts in September 1978. They provide a longer-term perspective on the trends and cyclical performance of profits.

Here is our brief survey of these other earnings measures available for the S&P 500 on a quarterly basis:

- *Reported (GAAP) earnings (S&P data since 1935).* Standard & Poor's has compiled S&P 500 quarterly earnings on a reported basis since the first quarter of 1935 (*Fig. 9*). The Securities and Exchange Commission (SEC) requires that publicly traded companies include financial statements in their (unaudited) 10-Q and (audited) 10-K reports, including earnings figures based on Generally Accepted Accounting Principles (GAAP).

  Interestingly, the long-term annual growth rate of reported earnings has mostly been around 6.0% and ranged between 5.0% and 7.0% since the start of the data.

- *Operating earnings (Standard & Poor's data since 1988).* Since the first quarter of 1988, Standard & Poor's has provided an operating version of the quarterly earnings of the S&P 500 companies (*Fig. 10*). Unlike the reported earnings series, it excludes one-time write-offs, charges, and gains. Both are available on a per-share basis as well as on a total-dollars aggregate basis.

  The operating measure almost always exceeds the reported one because one-time unusual costs and losses tend to occur more frequently than one-time windfall gains. S&P's in-house analysts determine the one-offs that are excluded from each of the 500 companies' reported earnings when compiling the operating earnings series for the S&P 500.

- *Operating earnings (I/B/E/S data since 1993).* To complicate matters, other widely respected data vendors calculate S&P 500 operating earnings somewhat differently than does Standard & Poor's. The most widely used numbers are compiled by Bloomberg, FactSet, I/B/E/S, and Zacks. Joe and I prefer the longer history of the I/B/E/S series.

The data in both the I/B/E/S and Standard & Poor's series are on a pro forma basis, so they reflect the composition of the S&P 500's portfolio as it was in each period. As a result, changes in the value of the index over time is an exercise in apples-to-oranges comparison: The value of today's index is being compared to the values of past versions of the index, even though its composition changes over time as companies are added, subtracted, merged, and acquired through the years.

The I/B/E/S measure tends to be the same as the comparable Standard & Poor's series but has diverged at times. Particularly during recessions, I/B/E/S operating earnings tends to well exceed Standard & Poor's measure because it treats more of the losses incurred during bad times as one-off (*Fig. 11*).

For example, according to I/B/E/S, the S&P 500 Energy sector had operating earnings of $3.04 per share during the first quarter of 2020, while Standard & Poor's calculated a loss of $9.16. Oil prices dropped sharply during the quarter. Standard & Poor's included the revaluation (or write-down) of the oil reserves. Neither I/B/E/S nor industry analysts did so in either their estimates or actual results. A similar plunge in oil prices caused a divergence between the Standard & Poor's and I/B/E/S operating earnings calculations for the Energy sector from the first quarter of 2015 through the second quarter of 2016.

So, the big difference between the Standard & Poor's and I/B/E/S measures of operating earnings per share is that the former determines which one-time items to exclude, while the latter is based on majority rule. In other words, it is based on the industry analysts' consensus on operating earnings, which tends to be the same as the operating numbers reported by the companies in their quarterly filings.

Obviously, company managements prefer to determine their own non-GAAP measure of operating earnings and are more favorably disposed toward industry analysts who follow their guidance. The SEC has warned some companies not to hype up their operating results by excluding bad stuff that shouldn't be excluded. Importantly, industry analysts and investors who are after the unvarnished truth can always analyze the results based on GAAP, which must be reported in the quarterly filings and reconciled back to any non-GAAP measures presented. Not surprisingly, the net write-offs tend to be greater for the I/B/E/S measure of operating earnings than for the one compiled by S&P (*Fig. 12*).

Some strategists disparage the concept of operating earnings, calling it "EBBS," or "earnings before bad stuff." They insist that reported earnings is the only correct measure. We prefer following both measures, knowing that reported earnings tend to diverge the most from operating earnings during downturns and bounce back when operations are back to normal.

Nevertheless, even during normal times, the I/B/E/S measure of operating earnings tends to exceed the S&P measure of operating earnings. One major reason is that Standard & Poor's doesn't agree with the relatively widespread practice, especially among technology companies and the analysts who cover them, of excluding stock option compensation as an expense when calculating operating earnings.

We believe that the stock market reflects the I/B/E/S measure of operating earnings since most industry analysts follow the guidance provided by company managements for what is considered to be one-time bad stuff. That's why all our work on the S&P 500's Earnings Squiggles, forward earnings, and the earnings valuation multiple is based on I/B/E/S data.

Revenues, Earnings, and Profit Margins

We started this primer with the stock market equation. Now let's examine the earnings equation, which simply states that earnings per share (E) equals revenues per share (R) multiplied by the profit margin (E/R):

$$E = E/R \times R$$

The actual quarterly data for S&P 500 revenues per share are reported by Standard & Poor's several weeks after the end of each quarter. Unlike for earnings, this is the only series for tracking actual revenues.

We use the same approach to calculate forward revenues as we use for forward earnings (i.e., taking the time-weighted average of analysts' expectations during the current year and the coming one). With both forward earnings and forward revenues in hand, we can also derive the implied S&P 500 profit margin. Dividing analysts' expectations for earnings by their expectations for revenues allows us to impute a series for the forward profit margin of the S&P 500. The monthly data for forward revenues start during January 2004, while the weekly series is available since mid-January 2006.

As we noted above, forward earnings per share tends to be a very good leading indicator of the four-quarter sum of actual operating earnings per share during economic expansions. Similarly, we've found that the monthly and weekly forward-revenues-per-share series are excellent coincident indicators of quarterly actual revenues per share, annualized simply by multiplying the series by 4.0 (*Fig. 13*). Not surprisingly, the implied weekly forward profit margin is also a very good coincident indicator of the actual quarterly profit margin (*Fig. 14*).

While the consensus annual estimated Earnings Squiggles tend to decline, as noted above, the slopes of the annual estimated revenues squiggles tend to be more predictable. We have 15 years of complete annual revenues squiggles from 2005 through 2019, with 25 months of data for each one of them (*Fig. 15*). We also have weekly revenues squiggles starting in January 19, 2006 (*Fig. 16*).

From the beginning to the end of each annual squiggle, using the monthly data, revenues estimates fell for six of the years and rose for nine (2005, 2006, 2007, 2008, 2011, 2012, 2017, 2018, and 2019) (*Fig. 17*). As with Earnings Squiggles, the steepest downward slopes in revenues squiggles occur during recessions, when analysts can't seem to cut estimates fast enough, while the steepest upward slopes are characteristic of economic recoveries—especially recoveries following recessions that were so bad that analysts became overly pessimistic.

The overall average revenues decline for the 25 months of the 15 years was –0.5%, with the six down years averaging –7.4% and the nine up years averaging 4.1%. For comparison purposes, Earnings Squiggles over the same 2005–2019 period averaged –7.2%, with the up five years averaging a gain of 6.8% and the 10 down years a decline of 14.1%.

Again, we observe that S&P 500 forward revenues per share is an excellent coincident indicator of actual quarterly S&P 500 revenues per share. It has been a very useful economic indicator for us. That's because both the actual quarterly data and the forward data are highly correlated with manufacturing and trade sales, as well as numerous other cyclical economic indicators including both the

Index of Coincident Economic Indicators (CEI) and the Index of Leading Economic Indicators (LEI) (*Fig. 18*). The same can be said about S&P 500 forward earnings per share: It too is highly correlated with both the CEI and LEI (*Fig. 19* and *Fig. 20*).

(For a handy table listing the various S&P 500 measures of earnings and revenues that we have discussed so far, along with their start dates, see *Appendix 2: S&P 500 Price Index, Revenues & Earnings Data Series.*)

NIPA Profits Comparisons

What about the quarterly profits statistics that the BEA compiles along with GDP in the NIPA? How do these profits data compare to the quarterly ones compiled by S&P for the S&P 500 firms? Economists tend to focus their attention on the NIPA profits series while mostly ignoring the S&P profits measure. That's because the NIPA series is deemed to be more comprehensive, which it is. However, NIPA can misrepresent what is happening to profits more so than the S&P 500 earnings data do.

To complicate the comparison of the two, the NIPA measure comes in two varieties. NIPA "book profits" is based on the results reported on a financial reporting basis. The alternative measure is "profits from current production." It is adjusted to restate the historical-cost basis used in profits tax accounting for inventory withdrawals and depreciation to the current-cost measures used in GDP. It is necessary to make these adjustments to calculate profits' contribution to GDP and to the share of National Income.

As noted above, S&P 500 quarterly profits data also come in two varieties, i.e., reported and operating. While the latter reflects net write-offs, it is never adjusted to derive a current production measure. The NIPA series isn't adjusted for net write-offs to derive an operating version of NIPA profits. Therefore, we believe that it makes the most sense to compare S&P 500 reported earnings to NIPA book profits, both on an after-tax basis (*Fig. 21*). Since 1965, the former has tended to average around 50% of the latter (*Fig. 22*).

So what else besides the earnings of the S&P 500 companies is included in NIPA book profits? According to the *NIPA Handbook*, corporate profits includes all US public, private, and "S" corporations.[5] It also includes other organizations that do not file federal corporate tax returns—such as certain mutual financial institutions and cooperatives, nonprofits that primarily serve business, Federal Reserve banks, and federally sponsored credit agencies. Most of the difference between the NIPA measure of profits and the S&P measure is attributable to sub-chapter S corporations and private corporations.

On its website, the Internal Revenue Service explains the difference between C and S corporations:

> A C corporation is taxed on its earnings, and then the shareholder is taxed when earnings are distributed as dividends. S corporations elect to pass corporate income, losses, deductions and credits through to their shareholders for federal tax purposes. Shareholders of S corporations report the pass-through of income and losses on their personal tax returns and are assessed tax at their individual income tax rates. This allows S corporations to avoid double taxation on the corporate income.[6]

As a result, most of the income of S corporations is paid out as dividends. Since S corporations tend to distribute most of their earnings to their limited number of shareholders as dividends, which are then taxed as personal income, they boost corporate profits even though they actually directly benefit the owners of the S corporations.

This helps to explain why NIPA's effective corporate tax rate has been well below the statutory rate. Furthermore, it suggests that S corporations have had a significant impact on exaggerating corporate profit's share of National Income, assuming as we do that S corporation dividends are more like labor compensation than profits.

Our conclusion is that comparing NIPA profits and S&P 500 earnings is like comparing apples and oranges. Actually, the NIPA measure is more like a fruit cocktail with lots of different fruit juices. For those of us in the stock market, what matters is the trend in the earnings of the S&P 500. (See *Appendix 3: Slicing and Dicing the NIPA Measure of Corporate Profits.*)

Chapter 2
S&P 500 Valuation

Flying with the Blue Angels

Industry analysts provide the earnings estimates that are discounted in stock prices. Investors determine the valuation of those earnings. While forward earnings isn't an infallible measure of earnings for forecasting purposes, we are convinced that the market is discounting the time-weighted average of analysts' consensus earnings expectations for the current year and the coming year. In our analysis of the stock market equation, we can specify that "E" is S&P 500 forward earning per share. "P" is the S&P 500 stock price index. "P/E" is the ratio of the S&P 500 stock price index to the S&P 500 forward earnings per share. Industry analysts' consensus expectations are used to derive the forward E, and investors determine the forward P/E.

We devised our "Blue Angels" chart framework to monitor these three variables in a visually useful way. In the monthly version, we multiply the S&P 500's forward earnings per share by hypothetical forward P/Es of 5.0 to 25.0 in increments of 5.0 (*Fig. 23*). The result is five different time series of an implied S&P 500 index price at the various P/E levels. They move in a parallel formation and never collide, just like the vapor trails left behind the Navy's famous Blue Angels jets.[7]

Superimposing the actual S&P 500 stock price index shows when it is breaking into new valuation territory, i.e., changing P/E "altitude" by moving toward a new higher or lower P/E series trail. In our presentations to clients, we often refer to the S&P 500 series as "the stunt plane flying through the vapor trails of the Blue Angels." The same framework can be constructed using weekly data to keep a more frequent watch on the Blue Angels relationships among P, E, and P/E (*Fig. 24*).

As the S&P 500 ascends or descends through the Blue Angels, we can see how much of the move is attributable to forward earnings versus the forward P/E. Generally, S&P 500 forward earnings per share isn't as volatile as the index's forward P/E. So big short-term moves in the stock index most often reflect changes in the forward P/E that cause the index to climb or fall toward the next Blue Angel P/E vapor trail. Conversely, moves in the actual index price that do not bring it closer to a nearby Blue Angel P/E altitude confirm that changes in the earnings outlook are driving the S&P 500's price action.

Forward earnings per share tends to rise fastest during economic recoveries and to fall fastest during recessions. Our simple Blue Angels framework clearly shows that bull markets typically occur when forward earnings and forward valuation are rising. Bear markets, when the S&P 500 is down 20% or more, typically occur when both are falling. Short-term bull-market selloffs of 10% to less than 20%, a.k.a. corrections, occur when valuation declines while forward earnings continues to rise. There was a rare bear market in 1987 when the forward P/E fell sharply while forward earnings continued to rise.

The bottom line is that we use Earnings Squiggles and Blue Angels as tools to benchmark our own forecasts to the earnings expectations and the valuation levels that the market is discounting. We monitor the trends of earnings expectations for the current year and next year as well as for forward earnings. We watch to see how much altitude the S&P 500 "stunt plane" is gaining or losing as a result of changes in forward earnings and valuation. These tools are like our air traffic control system, providing us with guidance through market turbulence.

So, for example, in the bull market from March 2009 to February 2020, as in the previous one from 2003 through 2007, we stayed bullish during stock price swoons when we saw that forward earnings was still rising. We anticipated a correction in early 2020 because the valuation multiple seemed high to us when it rose to 19.0, matching the P/E just before the big correction in late 2018.[8] We turned bullish on March 25, 2020, anticipating that the Fed's latest round of monetary easing would boost the P/E, with stock prices rising faster than earnings were falling, as discussed in the next chapter.

So, what we actually do for a living is this: We forecast the forecast. We predict where forward earnings will be at the end of the current year and the coming year. That amounts to forecasting next year's and the following year's earnings since those will be the forward earnings at the end of the current year and the coming year, assuming that industry analysts eventually will concur with our earnings outlook. Of course, it doesn't end there. To convert our forecasts for forward earnings per share to S&P 500 targets at the end of the current year and the coming year, we also need to forecast where the forward P/E will be at both points in time.

In the Eyes of the Beholder

As an economist, I've always felt relatively comfortable with predicting earnings, since they are mostly determined by the performance of the economy. Assessing the outlook for the P/E is the tougher of the two variables to forecast, in my opinion.

Judging valuation in the stock market is akin to judging a beauty contest. Episode 42 of the television series *The Twilight Zone* is titled "Eye of the Beholder." It's about a woman who undergoes her 11th and last legally allowed facelift to correct her looks, as required by the totalitarian regime. When the bandage is removed, the doctors are disappointed and can barely hide their disgust: She is still beautiful. Then the camera reveals the faces of the doctors and nurses. They look horrifying to us viewers, with their pig-like snouts, though clearly pleasing to one another. The beautiful misfit escapes with a handsome man to a village of their "own kind," where the rest of society won't be subjected to their repellent good looks. "Beauty is in the eye of the beholder," the man tells the woman.

Not only is beauty subjective, Hollywood tells us, but it can be dangerous. At the end of the original version of the movie *King Kong* (1933), the big ape's death is blamed by his handler on Ann Darrow, Kong's blond love interest, played by Fay Wray: "It was beauty that killed the beast."

Valuation is in the eye of the beholder too. And buying stocks when they are most loved and very highly valued can also be deadly. For example, during the late 1990s, investors scrambled to purchase high-tech stocks in the United States. At the height of the frenzy, the S&P 500 Information Technology sector accounted for a record 33.7% of the market capitalization of the entire S&P 500 but only 18.2% of its earnings (*Fig. 25*). The forward P/E of the S&P 500 peaked at a record 24.5 during July 1999, led by a surge in the forward P/E of the S&P 500 Information Technology sector to a record high of 48.3 during March 2000 (*Fig. 26*). When that bubble burst, many tech investors suffered crushing losses in their portfolios as the sector's price index did not make another new high for 18 years.

Stocks tend to rise along a long-term trend line that is determined by the long-term growth rate of earnings. Since 1979, the trend growth rate for S&P 500 forward earnings on a monthly basis has ranged between 6% and 7% (*Fig. 27*). Nevertheless, a long-term investor who hopes to earn this projected return may earn less if stocks are bought when they are overvalued and earn more if stocks are bought when undervalued. A short-term trader doesn't care about long-term returns, but buy-and-hold investors should care about buying stocks when they are relatively cheap rather than too expensive.

How can we judge whether stock prices are too high, too low, or just right? Investment strategists are fond of using stock valuation models to do so. Some of these are simple. Some are complex. The levels, changes, and growth rates in numerous variables—such as earnings, dividends, inflation, interest rates, and various risk metrics—all are thrown into the pot to cook up a "fair value" for the stock market. If the stock market's price index exceeds the number indicated by the model, then the market is overvalued. If it is below fair value, then stocks are undervalued. As a rule, investors should buy when stocks are undervalued and should sell, or hold off buying, when they are overvalued.

A model can help us to assess value. But models by their very nature are attempts to simplify reality, which is always a great deal more complex and unpredictable. Valuation is ultimately a judgment call. It tends to be controversial, since everyone has their own opinion on what's a pig of a stock and what's a knockout at various levels of valuation.

Valuation is not only subjective; it's also relative.

Stocks are cheap or dear relative to other assets, such as bonds, for example. There are no absolutes. Even this statement is controversial since some observers swear by a reversion-to-the-mean approach, which compares stock valuation to its historical average rather than to other asset classes. When the P/E is above the historical mean, they warn that stocks are overvalued and vulnerable to reverting to the mean.

These diehards ignore all other factors that may be boosting valuations, and occasionally die waiting to be proven that they were right after all. It's been said that history doesn't repeat itself, but it rhymes. Similarly, history shows that valuation multiples do eventually revert to their means, though only briefly as they transition from overvalued to undervalued and back. Insights into how much time they might linger above and below their means, and the magnitude of the deviations, are not provided by simple reversion-to-the-mean models, which also don't consider that means can change over time along with inflation and interest rates.

Reversion to the Mean

Of the various reversion-to-the-mean models, it's the deviation of the forward P/E from its mean that we favor the most when we assess valuation. But the exercise is still a beauty contest. Common sense strongly suggests that the best time to buy stocks is when forward P/Es are low, while the best time to sell is when P/Es are high. However, doing so is not that simple. Stocks seemed relatively expensive in late 1996, which is why Federal Reserve Board Chair Alan Greenspan famously asked the valuation question in a December 5, 1996 speech: "But how do we know when irrational exuberance has unduly escalated asset values, which then become subject to unexpected and prolonged contractions, as they have in Japan over the past decade?"[9]

Right before posing the question, he suggested that stocks were not irrationally exuberant given that "sustained low inflation implies less uncertainty about the future, and lower risk premiums imply higher prices of stocks and other earning assets." The S&P 500 proceeded to soar 106.5% for another three years, from December 6, 1996, through March 24, 2000, led by a bubble in technology stocks. Lots of money can be made during bubbles, if you know enough to get out at the top.

Another issue regarding forward P/E data for the S&P 500 is that it's available only from September 1978. More years of data are necessary to determine whether the valuation multiple is high or low within an historical context. Besides, more data might suggest other testable models of valuation. As noted in the previous chapter, there are other earnings series of actual results—on both reported and operating bases and going back much further than forward earnings—that can be used to construct other reversion-to-the-mean models. Often, these models are based on four-quarter moving sums of the earnings series. In other words, trailing earnings are used to calculate trailing P/Es.

The advocates of trailing earnings models do have the choice of using either reported earnings or operating earnings (i.e., excluding one-time extraordinary gains and losses). Of course, more pessimistically inclined investment strategists focus on reported earnings, the lower of the two measures. Whichever is used, the data are available only on a quarterly basis with a lag of three to six weeks, limiting the usefulness of a trailing earnings approach. In any event, stock prices should be based on expected earnings, not trailing earnings, in our opinion. Forward earnings data reflect expectations and are available on a timelier basis, though with less history than trailing earnings. Models with P/Es based on trailing earnings often produce valuation conclusions quite different from those of models with P/Es based on forward expected earnings.

Using monthly data dating back to 1989, let's compare the valuation multiples of the S&P 500 when using forward earnings, trailing operating earnings, and trailing reported earnings. The P/Es based on trailing earnings—both operating and reported—always exceed the measure based on forward earnings. And the P/E based on trailing reported earnings always exceeds the P/E based on trailing operating earnings (*Fig. 28*). Given that they are using past earnings, trailing P/Es tend to imply overvaluation well ahead of forward P/Es, so investment strategists relying on trailing earnings tend to turn bearish too early in bull markets. The most bearishly inclined of them tend to favor the trailing P/E based on reported earnings because it is the most pessimistic of the bunch.

To be fair, when recessions hit, forward earnings expectations turn out to be too high and are slashed, confirming with the benefit of hindsight that forward P/Es were too high. The bears tend to growl, "We told you so."

Joe and I do track all the measures of the P/E both in absolute terms and relative to their means, along with similar valuation ratios deemed to be mean reverting. However, we don't buy the idea that the mean is determined by the laws of nature and exerts some sort of inherent gravitational pull on valuation, surrounding it with a force field that deflects all other influences. While the simple reversion-to-the-mean models are worth tracking, in our view, we recognize that they ignore how changes in interest rates, inflation, and technologies might impact valuation on short-term and long-term bases.

In any event, we've constructed a P/E series that starts in 1935 using S&P 500 quarterly trailing reported earnings through 1978, monthly forward earnings from January 1979 through April 1994, then weekly forward earnings (*Fig. 29*). The mean of this patchwork has been around 15.0. The series shows that its usefulness as a market-timing tool leaves much to be desired. It can take a long time to revert to the mean both on the way up and on the way down. On the other hand, this P/E series did show that stocks were cheap relative to the mean in the early 1980s, expensive in the late 1990s, and cheap again during the late 2000s.

Another valuation measure favored by the reversion-to-the-mean crowd is the ratio of the value of all stocks traded in the US to nominal Gross National Product (GNP), which is nominal Gross Domestic Product (GDP) plus net income receipts from the rest of the world. The data for the numerator are included in the Fed's quarterly *Financial Accounts of the United States*; that report lags the GNP report, which is available on a preliminary basis a couple of weeks after the end of a quarter. They aren't exactly timely data.

This ratio has been widely followed ever since Warren Buffett highlighted it in an essay for the December 2001 *Fortune*: "For me, the message of that chart is this: If the percentage relationship falls to the 70% or 80% area, buying stocks is likely to work very well for you. If the ratio approaches 200%—as it did in 1999 and a part of 2000—you are playing with fire."[10]

We can construct both monthly and weekly proxies for the Buffett Ratio. The S&P 500 stock price index can be divided by S&P 500 forward revenues per share instead of forward earnings per share. This forward price-to-sales ratio (P/S) closely tracks the Buffett Ratio (*Fig. 30* and *Fig. 31*). However, this forward P/S ratio is very highly correlated with the forward P/E ratio, so it doesn't bring much additional value to assessing valuation (*Fig. 32*). And neither does the Buffett Ratio for that matter.

Fundamentals Matter

A closer look at our P/E series since 1935 shows that the mean since then doesn't mean much, since inflation and interest rates likely influenced the valuation multiple. The P/E was generally below the historical average when inflation and interest rates were rising toward historically high levels. It was generally above the average when inflation and interest rates were falling toward historically low levels (*Fig. 33* and *Fig. 34*). These fundamental factors obviously matter in the determination of valuation. Valuation isn't all about reversion to the mean!

Many years ago, from the late 1970s through the late 1990s, there was a reasonably good correlation between the 10-year US Treasury bond yield and the S&P 500 forward earnings yield, which is simply the reciprocal of the forward P/E (*Fig. 35*). In 1997, I called this relationship the "Fed's Stock Valuation Model" (FSVM), and the name stuck. I must have cursed it, since it hasn't worked as a useful valuation model or market-timing tool since the early 2000s. The FSVM has been signaling that stocks are increasingly cheap relative to bonds since the early 2000s (*Fig. 36*). The FSVM certainly didn't provide any warning ahead of the grizzly bear market caused by the Great Financial Crisis.

Maybe it is starting to work again now.

The model showed that stocks were undervalued relative to bonds by a record 88% during the week of August 7, 2020. After all, the Treasury bond's record-low yield of 0.50% on August 4 implied a P/E for the bond of 200 (!), using the reciprocal of the yield. In other words, the FSVM was clearly signaling the S&P 500's forward P/E was too low relative to the bond's P/E. Take that for what it's worth, considering that it is just as easy to argue that bonds were ridiculously overvalued relative to stocks. The truth presumably lay somewhere in between—i.e., stocks were relatively cheap, while bonds were relatively expensive.

Now let's examine the impact of inflation on valuation. The earnings yield of the S&P 500, which is simply the reciprocal of the P/E based on reported earnings, is well correlated with the consumer price index (CPI) inflation rate on a year-over-year basis (*Fig. 37*). The real earnings yield (REY) of the S&P 500 is the difference between the nominal yield and the CPI inflation rate (*Fig. 38*). The result is a mean-reversion valuation model that logically includes inflation.

The average of the real yield since 1952 is 3.19%. The model tends to anticipate bear markets when the yield falls close to zero. John Apruzzese, the chief investment officer of Evercore Wealth Management, examined this model in his November 2017 paper, *A Reality Check for Stock Valuations*.[11] Based on the REY model, he found that "stocks appear more reasonably priced than the conventional P/E ratio suggests during periods of low inflation and rising markets, and more expensive during periods of high inflation and falling markets when they otherwise might seem cheap."

Another fundamental factor that needs to be considered is the analysts' consensus expected long-term earnings growth rate (LTEG) for the S&P 500. I/B/E/S provides a series for LTEG—i.e., average projected annual earnings growth over the next five years (*Fig. 39*). It's available on a monthly basis since 1995 and on a weekly basis since 2006. It has been quite volatile considering that it is supposed to measure consensus expectations for the long-term trend in earnings growth. In the previous chapter, we observed that both reported quarterly earnings since 1935 and forward operating earnings since 1979 have ranged between 5% and 7% annualized growth trends.

So how can we explain why the monthly measure of LTEG has ranged between a low of 9.3% and a high of 18.7% with a mean of 12.6% from 1995 through the end of 2019? Keep in mind that LTEG is based on analysts' expectations for the long-term earnings growth of the companies they follow, not for the overall S&P 500. Their optimistic bias toward the future of their companies is clearly reflected in LTEG.

In addition, as was evident during the second half of the 1990s, industry analysts justified the run-up in tech stock prices by raising their LTEG expectations from 16.7% in January 1995 to a record high of 28.7% during October 2000 (*Fig. 40*). When the tech bubble burst, LTEG reversed course. It was pushed further downward again by the Great Financial Crisis. It was back on the ascent from 2017 through the first half of 2018, when industry analysts anticipated that President Donald Trump's pro-business policies—including less regulation and lower corporate tax rates—would be bullish for LTEG. But then during the second half of 2018 through 2019, Trump's escalating trade wars caused LTEG to tumble, and the *coup de grâce* was provided the following year by the Great Virus Crisis.

We can use the monthly and weekly LTEG series to construct a PEG (or P/E to long-term earnings growth) ratio for the S&P 500. It is equal to the forward P/E divided by LTEG (*Fig. 41* and *Fig. 42*). Conceptually, using a PEG ratio for valuation purposes makes lots of sense. When long-term investors buy stocks, they aren't focusing on expected earnings just over the coming year but rather over the next several years. The higher the expected growth in earnings, the more dearly an investor is likely to value a stock.

However, what makes sense for an individual stock may not be as sensible for the overall market.

Overall earnings growth is limited by the nominal growth rate of overall revenues, which depends on the growth of nominal global economic activity. If earnings growth expectations for the overall market well exceed the growth potential of the global economy, that would be a sign of irrational exuberance rather than justification for paying an inflated P/E well above an inflated LTEG. So while tech P/Es seemed to be justified by rising LTEG for tech stocks during the late 1990s, they had more room to crash when LTEG was revised downward when the bubble burst.

In other words, the PEG measure is more likely to run into trouble at the sector level, where irrational exuberance may distort earnings growth expectations—as happened during the second half of the 1990s, when industry analysts raised their LTEG for technology. It seems to us that they were doing so mostly to justify the rapid ascent in prices. Even Fed Chairman Alan Greenspan justified high stock prices during the tech bull market by noting that industry analysts were raising their growth expectations. He said so in a September 5, 1997 speech at Stanford University: "And the equity market itself has been the subject of analysis as we attempt to assess the implications for financial and economic stability of the extraordinary rise in equity prices—a rise based apparently on continuing upward revisions in estimates of our corporations' already robust long-term earning prospects."[12]

What he forgot to mention is that this is exactly why irrational exuberance always ends badly. It attracts too much buzz, too much press, too many speculators, and most importantly too much capital that funds new competitors in the hot industry. While valuations are soaring, competition from new entrants starts to squeeze margins and saturates the market. Once investors recognize that analysts' earnings growth expectations are too optimistic, stockholders scramble to sell, causing P/Es to fall even faster than growth expectations.

Discipline of Dividends

The focus on valuing earnings is a relatively new phenomenon that started with the bull market of the 1990s. Before then, most valuation models for individual stocks focused on dividends, not earnings. Investors compared the dividend yield, not the current earnings yield, to the bond yield. Corporations were valued on their ability to pay and grow dividends, which represented a tangible return to investors. Retained earnings—profits after taxes and dividends—were reinvested in the business, presumably to increase the capacity of the corporation to pay more dividends in the future.

Investors could analyze the dividend payout history of a company. Then they could project a reasonable future payment stream to shareholders and calculate the present discounted value of the firm using a dividend-discount model (DDM). If the present discounted value was more than the share price in the market, then investors could expect to get a better-than-average return by investing in the company's stock. Of course, if the present discounted value of the projected future stream of dividends was less than the share price in the market, then prudent investors might sell the stock, or at least underweight it in their portfolios.

The simplest version of the DDM is the Gordon growth model, which assumes a constant rate of growth for a company's dividends (g). The fair value price (P) is calculated as the estimated value of next year's dividend (D) divided by (r - g), where r is the company's cost of capital:

$$P = D / (r - g)$$

This dividend-centric valuation discipline provided a powerful and conservative system of checks and balances for corporate managers. Dividends are cash payments. There is no way to print the money; it must be available from a company's cash flow. Managers were under pressure to deliver dividend growth, but they also had to retain enough of their earnings to reinvest in their companies that dividends would continue to grow.

This conservative but disciplined system was replaced during the bull market of the 1990s by a more freewheeling approach to valuation that was more easily abused to boost stock prices to levels that could never be justified by dividends. Indeed, many companies, especially those that seemed to be growing rapidly, reduced their dividend payouts or eliminated them entirely. More earnings were retained, and fewer dividends were paid out to investors.

The rationale in most cases seemed sensible: Growth companies experiencing rapid increases in their earnings could reinvest their profits and get a better long-term return for their investors through share-price appreciation as the companies expanded and became more valuable. Besides, investors couldn't reinvest the dividends on their own and still do as well as a growth company because they would have to pay taxes on the dividend income after it had already been taxed at the corporate level.

The new approach to valuation based on earnings rather than dividends was both a blessing and a curse. Under the dividend regime, most managers adopted a slow but steady and conservative approach. As long as dividends were growing, investors tended to be content with managements' performance. Growing dividends was a long-term process occasionally disrupted by economic downturns. Reinvesting retained earnings required a great deal of planning, and the projected returns had to be just high enough to boost dividends without subjecting the company to a great deal of risk.

Under the earnings-centric valuation regime, companies no longer faced the quarterly grind of delivering cash dividends. The cash could be plowed back into the business. Greater risk was acceptable because there was less pressure to deliver the cash to investors every quarter. This meant that managers could be more entrepreneurial. It also meant that some could abuse the system by artificially boosting their earnings. Managing earnings rather than managing the business became an increasing problem during the bull market of the 1990s.

Then-Fed Chair Alan Greenspan put the stock market bubble of the late 1990s into perspective on March 26, 2002, in a speech on corporate governance that he presented at New York University. Greenspan observed that shareholders' obsession with earnings was a relatively new phenomenon:

Prior to the past several decades, earnings forecasts were not
nearly so important a factor in assessing the value of corporations. In fact, I do not recall price-to-earnings ratios as a prom-
inent statistic in the 1950s. Instead, investors tended to value
stocks on the basis of their dividend yields.[13]

During 2002, many of the most abusive practices in managing earnings came to light as a consequence of numerous corporate accounting scandals. Undoubtedly, the system needed to be
reformed, and that was accomplished through the Sarbanes–Oxley
Act of 2002. The good news is that dividends have been making
a comeback since the financial crisis of 2008. As bond yields have
plunged since then, dividend-yielding stocks have come back into
favor, especially those of companies with a long record of raising
their dividends. We often show the power of dividends by calculating the current dividend yield of an S&P 500 portfolio pur-
chased in 1970, 1980, 1990, 2000, and 2010. By mid-2020, those
hypothetical portfolios were yielding 69.2%, 44.0%, 18.0%, 4.5%,
and 4.7%, respectively.

Unlike the forward earnings yield, or even the trailing earnings
yield, the dividend yield of the S&P 500 doesn't correlate enough
with either the 10-year US Treasury bond yield or the inflation rate
to inspire the construction of a valuation model (*Fig. 43*). As inflation soared from the 1950s through the 1970s, the bond yield rose
much faster than the dividend yield. During the disinflationary
1980s and 1990s, the bond yield fell faster than the dividend yield.
Since 2000, the dividend yield has been on a slight uptrend, while
the bond yield has continued to fall. Since the financial crisis of
2008, the bond yield and the dividend yield have been about the
same for the first time since the late 1950s.

We've extended our Blue Angels framework to track the relationship of the S&P 500 dividend and dividend yield to the S&P 500
stock price index (*Fig. 44*). The arithmetic relationship is simple:

$$P = D / Y$$

where P = the S&P 500 stock price index, D = aggregate dividends paid by the S&P 500 corporations, and Y = the dividend yield, or D/P.

The Blue Angels show the hypothetical value of the S&P 500 using the actual dividends paid out divided by dividend yields from 1.0% to 6.0%. The Blue Angels analysis reveals what's propelling the S&P 500's price performance. If the "plane" (index) is flying along a particular "vapor trail," then the flight path of dividend is determining the flight path of the plane (i.e., the S&P 500's stock price performance). Diversions above (below) a vapor trail indicate falling (rising) yields since investors are clearly paying more (less) for the same amount of dividend dollars thus changing the yield.

Currently, in September 2020, the conclusion of this Blue Angels analysis is that stocks are attractive relative to bonds because the dividend yield exceeds the bond yield, and the long-term uptrend in S&P 500 dividends has been roughly 6% since the end of 1946 (*Fig. 45*).

Chapter 3

The Framework in Good and Bad Times

Very Useful Indicators

In the first chapter, we observed that both the forward revenues and the forward earnings of the S&P 500 are very useful economic indicators because they correlate so well with lots of leading and coincident business cycle indicators in the US. They have been especially useful because they have a long history of availability, weekly since mid-January 2006 for forward revenues and weekly since the end of March 1994 for forward earnings.

Focusing on the forward earnings series, we see that during the six economic recessions since the late 1970s, it peaked just before the start of the downturns and bottomed near their troughs (*Fig. 46*). Forward earnings also confirms that there was a mid-cycle growth recession during 1985 and 1986. While there was a sharp selloff in the S&P 500 during October 1987, forward earnings continued to rise through 1989. The bull market of the 1990s was supported by a long uptrend in forward earnings. Forward earnings remained relatively flat following the recession of 2000 to 2002, but then it proceeded to make new record highs, as did the S&P 500, through late 2007. The next year found forward earnings tanking during the Great Financial Crisis (GFC).

A V-shaped recovery in forward earnings started in early 2009. The metric rose to a new record high during May 2011, after which its pace of rise slowed through mid-2014. It then stalled through mid-2016 as a result of a global economic slowdown.

But it started moving higher again at a quickening pace through 2017, signaling a pickup in global economic growth. It got another boost in early 2018 when the corporate tax rate was slashed from 35% to 21%. As increasing trade tensions between the US and its major trading partners, particularly China, slowed the global economy, forward earnings stalled once again during 2019 through early 2020. Then the Great Virus Crisis (GVC) hit.

A Tale of Two Crises

Now let's turn to how we used the analytical framework discussed so far to analyze and predict the likely impact of the GVC on the stock market equation. To do so, we benchmarked our outlook to the performance of forward revenues and earnings during the GFC.

The GFC to a large extent was a typical business cycle downturn. It was preceded by an economic boom that was led by speculative excesses, particularly in the housing industry. When that bubble burst, a credit crunch worsened the resulting recession, with real GDP falling 4.0% from the fourth quarter of 2007 through the second quarter of 2009. The Dating Committee of the National Bureau of Economic Research (NBER) ruled that it lasted 18 months, from December 2007 through June 2009.

The collapse of Lehman Brothers on Monday, September 15, 2008, was the major calamity that exacerbated the GFC. The S&P 500 had dropped 20.0% from its October 9, 2007 record high through the previous Friday close. The index was experiencing a garden-variety bear market up until that point. It turned into a great crash after Lehman failed, with the S&P 500 plunging another 46.0% through the bear market's bottom on March 9, 2009. The results were a global credit crunch and a severe global recession.

The declaration on March 11, 2020, of a pandemic by the World Health Organization (WHO) precipitated the GVC as governments around the world locked down their economies to slow the spread of the virus. The result was a severe global recession, as evidenced by freefalls in world production and in the volume of world exports comparable to those of the GFC.

However, the GVC is unique. In many ways, it's like a major natural disaster that hit the entire global economy. Initially, it did trigger a credit crunch as a pandemic of fear spread through the financial markets causing a mad dash for cash, which caused credit-quality yield spreads to widen dramatically and depressed stock prices. But the world's major central banks quickly halted the credit crunch by pouring lots of liquidity into global financial markets.

The NBER's Dating Committee determined that the US economy peaked during February 2020. Real GDP dropped 10.6% from the fourth quarter of 2019 through the second quarter of 2020. Numerous economic indicators bottomed during April as governments around the world started to ease lockdown restrictions. That would make it a two-month recession. A recession that short and severe is unprecedented, but that's because there is no precedent for a recession caused by government-mandated lockdowns around the world implemented to slow the spread of the virus.

We first sounded the alarm about COVID-19 in our Tuesday, January 28, 2020 *Morning Briefing* titled "Something to Fear." We wrote:

> Until Friday [January 24], there was nothing to fear but nothing to fear, other than historically high valuation multiples. Since Friday, there has been something else to fear: that the coronavirus outbreak in China is spreading rapidly and turning into a pandemic, i.e., a global epidemic. The S&P 500 dropped 0.9% on Friday and 1.6% yesterday. The most

unsettling news over the weekend was that people infected with the virus might show no symptoms for two weeks but still be contagious during that time.

The asymptomatic nature of the virus was our biggest concern compared to previous pandemics.

Nevertheless, the S&P 500 rebounded and continued to rise to a record high on February 19 (*Fig. 47*). That same morning, our commentary was titled "In a Good Place?" We observed that during his semi-annual congressional testimony reviewing monetary policy on February 11 and 12, Federal Reserve Chair Jerome Powell emphasized that the "US economy is in a very good place." The threat from the coronavirus is something to watch, he said, but too early to understand. Nevertheless, he affirmed that "there is no reason why the expansion can't continue." We wrote: "We wish he would stop using that expression [i.e., 'in a good place']. Our contrary instincts come out every time he says it."

From its record high on February 19, the S&P 500 proceeded to plunge 33.9% through March 23. On February 25, we wrote that the "Fed may need to deliver a couple more rate cuts to keep the US economy in a good place." Sure enough, the federal funds rate was cut on March 3 by 50 basis points to a range of 1.00%–1.25%.

We observed that a pandemic of fear was spreading in the financial markets faster than the viral pandemic. We started to write about the "mad dash for cash," as evidenced by soaring holdings of liquid assets, rapidly widening credit-quality spreads, and big outflows from bond mutual funds. In Zoom conference calls with our accounts, many told us that they wanted to rebalance their portfolios by selling some of their bonds and buying more stocks as they got cheaper, but the credit markets had frozen, making it very difficult to sell bonds without taking a huge hit.

The financial markets continued to melt down after the WHO officially declared the pandemic on March 11. On Sunday, March 15, the Fed held an emergency meeting of the Federal Open Market Committee and announced that the federal funds rate would be slashed by 100 basis points to 0.00%–0.25%. In addition, the central bank committed to a fourth program of quantitative easing (QE4) to purchase $700 billion of US Treasury and mortgage-backed securities.

On Monday, March 16, the S&P 500 dropped 12%. That partly reflected a vote of no confidence in the Fed's response to the pandemic. The Fed seemed to be running out of ammo for its monetary bazookas. Instead of having a shock-and-awe impact, the immediate reaction to the Fed's March 15 actions the next day was more like "aw, shucks!"

To be fair, that same day President Donald Trump pivoted from saying that COVID-19 was like a bad flu to saying that we should stay home if our state governors ordered us to do so. That was the gist of the new guidelines issued by the White House that day "for every American to follow over the next 15 days as we combat the virus." The governor of California issued a stay-in-place order on March 19; New York's governor followed on March 20, and the rest of the states' governors did the same over the following few days.

The stock market continued to fall, and credit-quality spreads soared. The Fed responded on March 23 with an open-ended commitment to buy US Treasury and mortgage-backed securities, and even to buy corporate bonds for the first time ever. We called it "QE4ever." The Fed had junked the bazookas, skipped the helicopters, and gone straight for the B-52 bombers to carpet-bomb the economy with cash. In our March 25 morning commentary, we wrote:

Yesterday's big rally in the stock market followed the Fed's announcement on Monday morning that QE4 was no longer limited to $700 billion but could extend to infinity and beyond. The Fed has turned into the Bank of Japan, offering an open-ended commitment to buy almost every financial asset forever, including investment grade corporate bonds. Joe and I think that Monday might have made the low in this bear market.

We predicted that the S&P 500 would be back in record-high territory during 2021. We didn't expect that it would get there by August 18, 2020, which is what happened. We observed that the year started out with investors still reaching for yield in the credit markets. The pandemic of fear quickly caused their mad dash for cash. Now, after QE4ever, we sensed a mad dash back into equities.

Following the WHO's declaration, we anticipated that analysts' S&P 500 consensus earnings expectations for 2020 and 2021 would freefall, bottoming by the middle of 2020, as we assumed that the lockdown restrictions would be gradually lifted by then. We also observed that because the GVC started in early 2020, investors would be giving more weight to 2021 expectations as 2020 progressed, as best measured by forward revenues and forward earnings; accordingly, as long as analysts expected a recovery by the coming year, both measures would likely bottom by mid-2020 and recover over the rest of the year through 2021.

On the other hand, the GFC worsened significantly near the end of 2008 following the collapse of Lehman. So it significantly depressed 2009 expectations for revenues and earnings. As a result, forward earnings didn't bottom until the week of May 8, 2009. That was 33 weeks after Lehman imploded. This time, forward earnings bottomed 10 weeks after the March 11 pandemic declaration (*Fig. 48*).

The stock market downdraft was longer and deeper during the GFC too. The S&P 500 fell 56.8% from its October 9, 2007 then-record high through March 9, 2009. This time, during the GVC, the S&P 500 dropped 33.9% from its then-record high on February 19, 2020 through March 23. It then rose to a new record high on August 18 and continued to rise through September 2, when we finished writing this primer.

Fed-Led Valuation Meltup

The surprise during the GVC was the big jump in the S&P 500's forward P/E from 12.9 on March 23 to 23.2 on September 2. With the benefit of hindsight, it all makes sense. The Fed's extraordinary policy responses to the GVC lowered the 10-year US Treasury bond yield below 1.00%. Credit-quality spreads narrowed significantly, resulting in record-low yields in investment-grade and high-yield corporate bonds. The forward P/E soared as investors scrambled to rebalance their portfolios out of bonds and into stocks. As a result, investors paid higher valuation multiples for stocks as yields fell closer to zero. The forward P/E soared along with the Fed's balance sheet (*Fig. 49*).

In our June 8 *Morning Briefing*, Joe and I observed that the stock market rally since March 23 could turn into the Mother of All Meltups (MAMU). Sure enough, between March 23 and September 2, the S&P 500 rose 60.0% to a new record high of 3580.84. It did so in 163 calendar days. The tech-heavy Nasdaq was up 75.7% over the same period, also to a new record high, of 12056.44.

The last time that the S&P 500 rebounded so strongly in such a short period was during September 1933. While the Nasdaq's rally was impressive, it paled by comparison to the 255.8% meltup from October 8, 1998 through March 10, 2000; but it seemed to be on the same trajectory as it was back then.

The forward P/E of the S&P 500 jumped to 23.2 by September 2, approaching its highs during the tech bubble of 1999. The forward price-to-sales ratio of the S&P 500 rose to 2.54 that same day, the highest on record.

Since late March, the stock market was working on answering the question that Joe and I started to ask as the meltup proceeded: "In a world of zero interest rates, what is the fair value of the S&P 500 forward P/E?" Taking our cue from Hamlet, we were simply asking whether stocks should be deemed to be—or not to be—too expensive when the federal funds rate is zero and the 10-year US Treasury bond yield is less than 1.00%, as both have been since the second half of March.

The market's answer was that stocks remained cheap as long as interest rates stayed near zero. The longer that was the case, the cheaper stock prices appeared to be and the higher they might potentially go. On August 27, Fed Chair Jerome Powell did his best to convince market participants that interest rates would stay close to zero for a very long time. He said so during his speech at the annual meeting hosted by the Federal Bank of Kansas City in Jackson Hole, Wyoming. He officially declared that the Fed no longer was aiming for a 2.0% bullseye on the inflation target but rather for an average around it.[14]

The 2.0% target was officially declared by the Fed in January 2012. During the 102 months since then through July 2020, the headline and core personal consumption expenditures deflator (PCED) inflation rates averaged 1.4% and 1.6%, rarely hitting the mark and consistently going below it. Since January 2012 through July 2020, the PCED has been tracking an annualized growth rate of 1.3%. As a result, it was 5.2% below where it should have been had it been tracking the Fed's 2.0% target. Undershooting the 2.0% inflation rate track since the start of 2012 by that great an amount left the Fed with plenty of room to tolerate a pickup in inflation without even "thinking about thinking about raising [interest] rates" under the new average-inflation-targeting (AIT) approach (quoting from Powell's July 29 press conference).[15]

Notwithstanding Powell's dovishness, bond yields initially rose in response to his speech. Investors seemed more concerned about the inflationary consequences of AIT than about the prospect that the federal funds rate will remain around zero for a longer time under the new regime. However, the fact that the Fed has failed to get inflation sustainably up to 2.0% since January 2012 raises the question of why the Fed would be any more likely finally to do so simply because it has declared that overshoots will be tolerated. In any event, if the bond yield continues to move higher, the Fed would likely adopt a policy of "yield-curve control," which is a fancy term for pegging the bond yield in a narrow range close to zero. In that scenario, the meltup in stock prices certainly would continue.

So again, we ask: In a world of zero interest rates, what is the fair value of the S&P 500 forward P/E? The market's answer at its then-record high on September 2 was as follows:

- *S&P 500 forward P/E.* The S&P 500's forward P/E on Wednesday, September 2 was 23.2, up from 12.9 on March 23. The last time it was this high was February 1, 2001, when the 10-year bond yield was 5.10% and the PCED inflation rate was 2.6%. The bond yield was down to 0.66% on September 2. July's PCED inflation rate was 1.0%.

- *S&P 500 Growth vs Value forward P/E.* As of the September 2 close, the forward P/E of the S&P 500 Growth index rose to 30.2, up from the March 23 low of 16.8 (*Fig. 50*). The latest reading is the highest since January 2001, when the bond yield was 5.16% and inflation was 2.6%.

The forward P/E of the S&P 500 Value index also jumped from 10.0 on March 23 to 17.4 on September 2. Interestingly, the ratio of the forward P/Es of Growth to Value has been on an uptrend since early 2017, and was at 1.74 on September 2, which is still well below this ratio's July 2000 bubble peak at a reading of 2.67. Meanwhile, the ratio of the forward earnings of Growth to Value had spiked higher since the start of 2020, explaining the widening P/E spread between the two.

- *S&P 5 vs S&P 495 forward P/E.* Leading the charge higher among the S&P 500 were the S&P 5. The Magnificent Five are the so-called FAAMG stocks (Facebook, Amazon, Apple, Microsoft, and Google). On September 2, they accounted for a record 27.2% of the market capitalization of the S&P 500. The market-cap share of the comparable S&P 5 during the tech bubble peaked at a then-record high of 18.5% during March 2000 (*Fig. 51*).

Collectively, the forward P/E of today's Magnificent Five rose to 64.6 on September 2 (*Fig. 52*). That might be justified by their ability to grow their forward revenues and earnings faster than the S&P 495 in a world of zero interest rates. By way of comparison, just before the S&P 500's tech bubble burst during March 2000, the sector's forward P/E peaked at 48.3, while the bond yield was 6.26% and inflation was 2.9%.

Just before we went to press, the S&P 500 sold off sharply after it hit its latest record high on September 2. The drop was led by the Magnificent Five, indicating that investors believed that they had been overvalued and that taking some profits made sense. Joe and I concluded that the selloff was a healthy correction. We hoped that the S&P 500 might stall, consolidating its gains since March 23 at least through the November 3 elections. That would give earnings some time to catch up with the stock market's rally. Before the market resumes its climb, investors might want to see more progress on the vaccine front, how the elections play out, and which letter of the alphabet best resembles the shape of the economic recovery. On the other hand, we didn't rule out the possibility of another 1999-style meltup.

While the stock market equation is a very simple one, there are always lots of factors that influence the outlook for earnings and the valuation of those earnings.

Epilogue

We hope you find that our primer on the stock market equation helps to inform a more structured understanding of the forces that drive the stock market.

Collectively, earnings tend to grow around 6% per year on average over the long run. In the short run, they tend to be procyclical, which means that they grow when the economy is growing and fall when the economy is heading into a recession. The market discounts analysts' consensus estimates for revenues and earnings this year and next year on a time-weighted basis. Calculating weekly forward revenues and forward earnings from analysts' estimates can provide very timely insights into the performance of the global economy as well as the underlying trends in quarterly revenues and earnings.

While we believe that our framework provides a disciplined approach to analyzing the macroeconomic fundamentals that are driving earnings, the valuation of those earnings by investors will continue to be much more subjective than objective. Nevertheless, there are fundamental factors that influence valuation multiples. Some, like inflation and interest rates, will always be important in assessing the valuation question. Other factors may be relatively new and worthy of careful analysis.

Long-term investors who purchase stocks when they are fairly valued can reasonably expect that S&P 500 earnings will continue to grow at its historical 6% annual rate. The S&P 500 closed at 3580.84 on September 2, 2020. A 6% annual appreciation rate, matching the growth rate of earnings, would take the index to

6168 by the end of 2029, a gain of 72%. That return will be higher or lower depending on whether the valuation multiple is higher or lower by the end of the decade than it was on September 2, 2020.

The S&P 500 has delivered solid returns for long-term investors in the past. It should continue to do so in the future.

Acknowledgments

Our colleagues at Yardeni Research deserve a great deal of credit for helping us to put this book together. Debbie Johnson and Mali Quintana spent countless hours checking the data that are shown in the book's text and charts. Melissa Tagg provided insightful research and fact-checking assistance. Jackie Doherty provided numerous good editorial suggestions. Mary Fanslau helped to administer the project. Geoff Moore and Steve Rybka delivered great tech support.

Our in-house editor, Sandra Cohan, cheerfully and masterfully pulled double duty by editing the book and our daily commentary. Her dedication to making the book happen was impressive.

Tom Clemmons also provided great editorial support. David Wogahn skillfully coordinated the production of the book.

Several professional friends also reviewed the manuscript and provided helpful guidance. They are John Apruzzese, Andrew Bell, Max King, and Howard Silverblatt.

Collectively, they provided many improvements; the authors take full responsibility for any remaining errors and omissions.

Appendices

1. *Deriving 12-Month Forward Earnings*
   https://www.yardenibook.com/pub/fevp-appendix1.pdf

2. *S&P 500 Price Index, Revenues & Earnings Data Series*
   https://www.yardenibook.com/pub/fevp-appendix2.pdf

3. *Slicing and Dicing the NIPA Measure of Corporate Profits*
   https://www.yardenibook.com/pub/fevp-appendix3.pdf

Author's Note

This study is another in a series of Topical Studies examining issues that I discussed in my book *Predicting the Markets: A Professional Autobiography* (2018) but in greater detail and on a more current basis. Previous studies in this series, which are available on my Amazon homepage, include:

Fed Watching for Fun & Profit: A Primer for Investors (2020)

Stock Buybacks: The True Story (2019)

The Yield Curve: What Is It Really Predicting? (2019)

The charts at the end of this study were current as of September 14, 2020. Updates (in color), as well as linked endnotes and appendices are available at **www.yardenibook.com/studies**.

Institutional investors are invited to sign up for the Yardeni Research service on a complimentary trial basis at **www.yardeni.com/trial-registration**.

Figures

Figure 1.

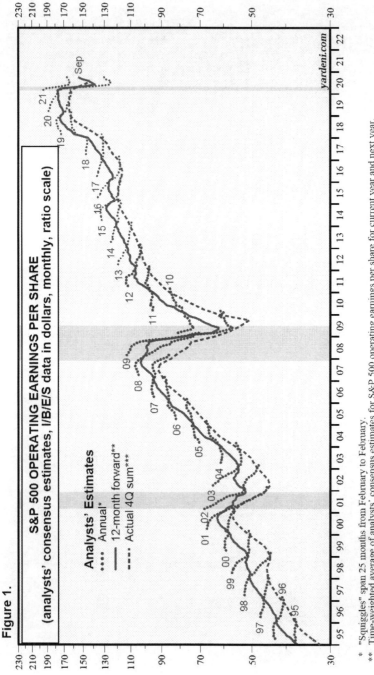

S&P 500 OPERATING EARNINGS PER SHARE
(analysts' consensus estimates, I/B/E/S data in dollars, monthly, ratio scale)

Analysts' Estimates
- - - - Annual*
───── 12-month forward**
- - - - Actual 4Q sum***

yardeni.com

* "Squiggles" span 25 months from February to February.
** Time-weighted average of analysts' consensus estimates for S&P 500 operating earnings per share for current year and next year.
*** Actual 4Q sum from I/B/E/S.
Note: Shaded areas are recessions according to the National Bureau of Economic Research.
Source: I/B/E/S data by Refinitiv.

Figure 2.

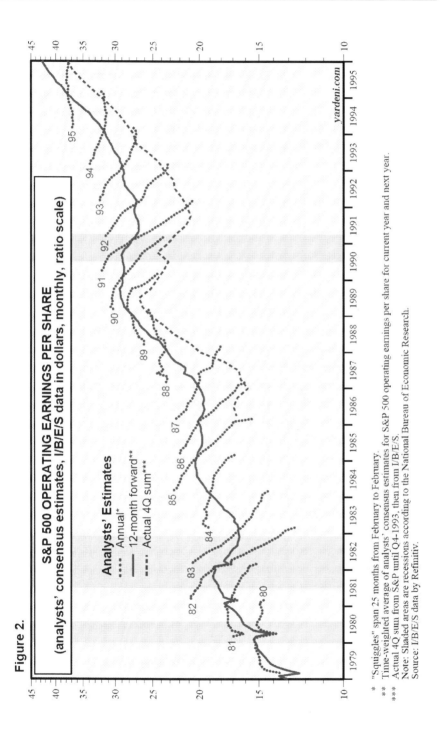

S&P 500 OPERATING EARNINGS PER SHARE
(analysts' consensus estimates, I/B/E/S data in dollars, monthly, ratio scale)

Analysts' Estimates
..... Annual*
——— 12-month forward**
- - - Actual 4Q sum***

yardeni.com

* "Squiggles" span 25 months from February to February.
** Time-weighted average of analysts' consensus estimates for S&P 500 operating earnings per share for current year and next year.
*** Actual 4Q sum from S&P until Q4-1993, then from I/B/E/S.
Note: Shaded areas are recessions according to the National Bureau of Economic Research.
Source: I/B/E/S data by Refinitiv.

Figure 3.

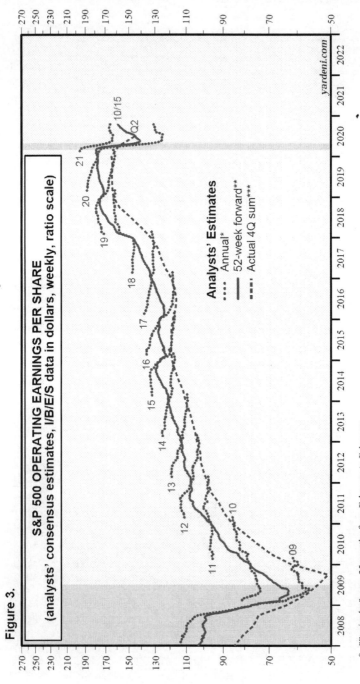

S&P 500 OPERATING EARNINGS PER SHARE
(analysts' consensus estimates, I/B/E/S data in dollars, weekly, ratio scale)

Analysts' Estimates
····· Annual*
——— 52-week forward**
-·-·- Actual 4Q sum***

yardeni.com

* "Squiggles" span 25 months from February to February.
** Time-weighted average of analysts' consensus estimates for S&P 500 operating earnings per share for current year and next year.
*** Actual 4Q sum from I/B/E/S.
Note: Shaded areas are recessions according to the National Bureau of Economic Research.
Source: I/B/E/S data by Refinitiv.

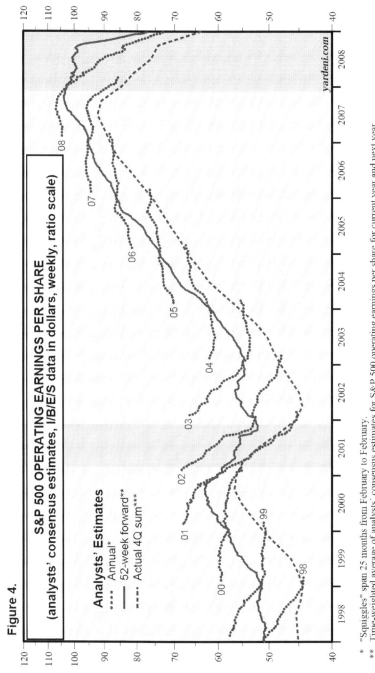

Figure 4.

S&P 500 OPERATING EARNINGS PER SHARE
(analysts' consensus estimates, I/B/E/S data in dollars, weekly, ratio scale)

Analysts' Estimates
•••• Annual*
—— 52-week forward**
- - - Actual 4Q sum***

yardeni.com

* "Squiggles" span 25 months from February to February.
** Time-weighted average of analysts' consensus estimates for S&P 500 operating earnings per share for current year and next year.
*** Actual 4Q sum from I/B/E/S.
Note: Shaded areas are recessions according to the National Bureau of Economic Research.
Source: I/B/E/S data by Refinitiv.

Figure 5.

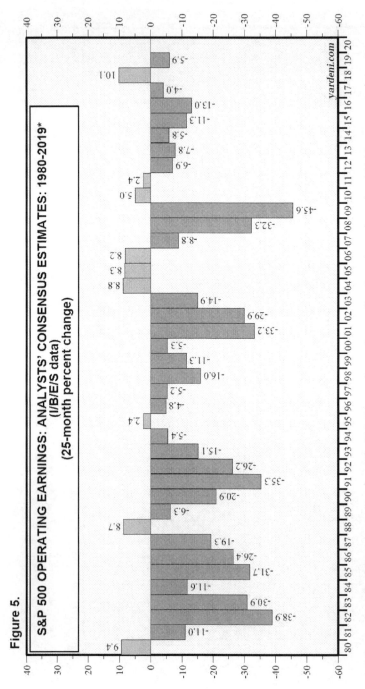

S&P 500 OPERATING EARNINGS: ANALYSTS' CONSENSUS ESTIMATES: 1980-2019*
(I/B/E/S data)
(25-month percent change)

yardeni.com

* Percent change in analysts' consensus estimates for S&P 500 operating earnings per share for each year shown from initial forecast to actual, e.g. from February 1979 to February 1981 for calendar year 1980.
Source: I/B/E/S data by Refinitiv.

Figure 6.

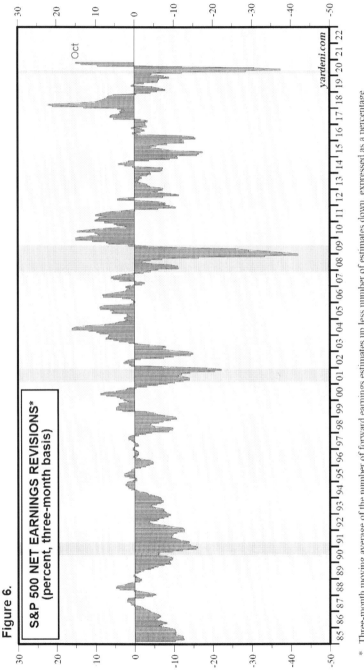

S&P 500 NET EARNINGS REVISIONS*
(percent, three-month basis)

yardeni.com

* Three-month moving average of the number of forward earnings estimates up less number of estimates down, expressed as a percentage of the total number of forward earnings estimates.
Note: Shaded areas are recessions according to the National Bureau of Economic Research.
Source: I/B/E/S data by Refinitiv.

Figure 7.

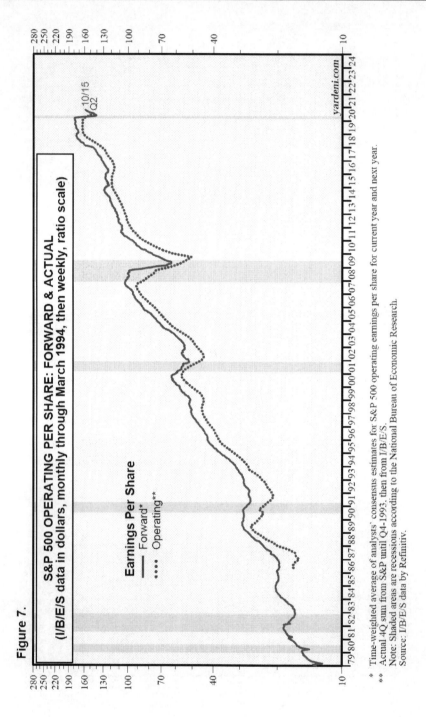

S&P 500 OPERATING PER SHARE: FORWARD & ACTUAL
(I/B/E/S data in dollars, monthly through March 1994, then weekly, ratio scale)

Earnings Per Share
— Forward*
····· Operating**

yardeni.com

* Time-weighted average of analysts' consensus estimates for S&P 500 operating earnings per share for current year and next year.
** Actual 4Q sum from S&P until Q4-1993, then from I/B/E/S.
Note: Shaded areas are recessions according to the National Bureau of Economic Research.
Source: I/B/E/S data by Refinitiv.

Figure 8.

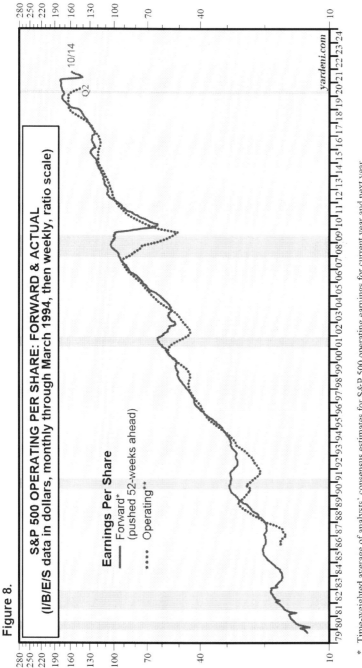

S&P 500 OPERATING PER SHARE: FORWARD & ACTUAL
(I/B/E/S data in dollars, monthly through March 1994, then weekly, ratio scale)

Earnings Per Share
— Forward*
(pushed 52-weeks ahead)
···· Operating**

yardeni.com

* Time-weighted average of analysts' consensus estimates for S&P 500 operating earnings for current year and next year.
** Actual 4Q sum from S&P until Q4-1993, then from I/B/E/S.
Note: Shaded areas are recessions according to the National Bureau of Economic Research.
Source: I/B/E/S data by Refinitiv.

Figure 9.

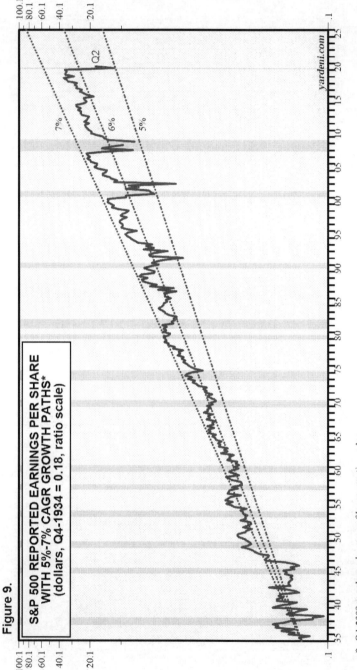

**S&P 500 REPORTED EARNINGS PER SHARE
WITH 5%-7% CAGR GROWTH PATHS***
(dollars, Q4-1934 = 0.18, ratio scale)

yardeni.com

* Q4-2008 not shown because of large negative value.
Note: Shaded areas are recessions according to the National Bureau of Economic Research.
Source: Standard & Poor's.

Figure 10.

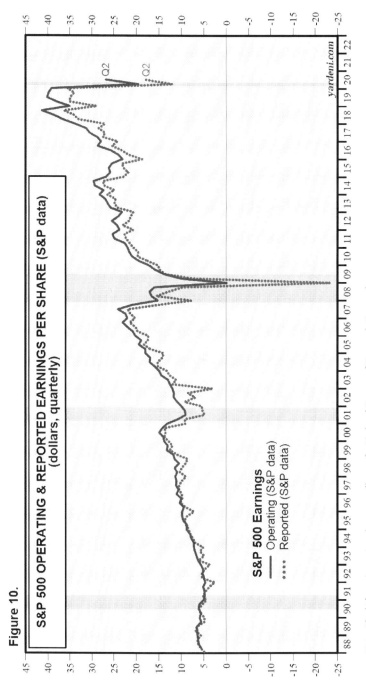

S&P 500 OPERATING & REPORTED EARNINGS PER SHARE (S&P data)
(dollars, quarterly)

S&P 500 Earnings
—— Operating (S&P data)
······ Reported (S&P data)

Note: Shaded areas are recessions according to the National Bureau of Economic Research.
Source: Standard & Poor's.

Figure 11.

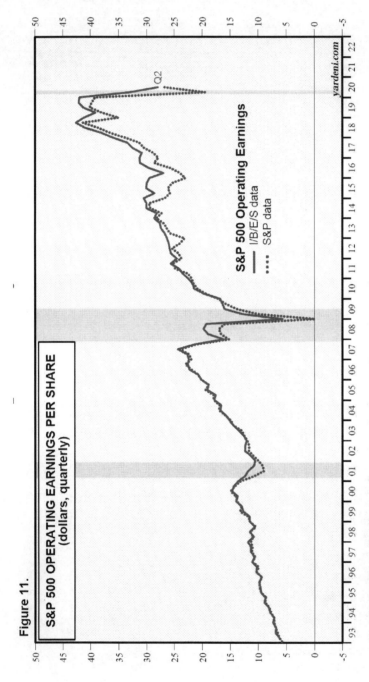

S&P 500 OPERATING EARNINGS PER SHARE
(dollars, quarterly)

S&P 500 Operating Earnings
—— I/B/E/S data
···· S&P data

Q2

yardeni.com

Note: Shaded areas are recessions according to the National Bureau of Economic Research.
Source: Standard & Poor's and I/B/E/S data by Refinitiv.

Figure 12.

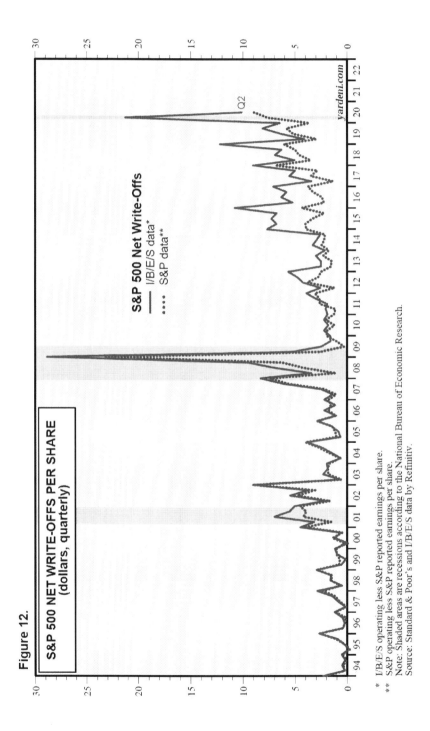

S&P 500 NET WRITE-OFFS PER SHARE
(dollars, quarterly)

S&P 500 Net Write-Offs
— I/B/E/S data*
.... S&P data**

*   I/B/E/S operating less S&P reported earnings per share.
** S&P operating less S&P reported earnings per share.
Note: Shaded areas are recessions according to the National Bureau of Economic Research.
Source: Standard & Poor's and I/B/E/S data by Refinitiv.

yardeni.com

Figure 13.

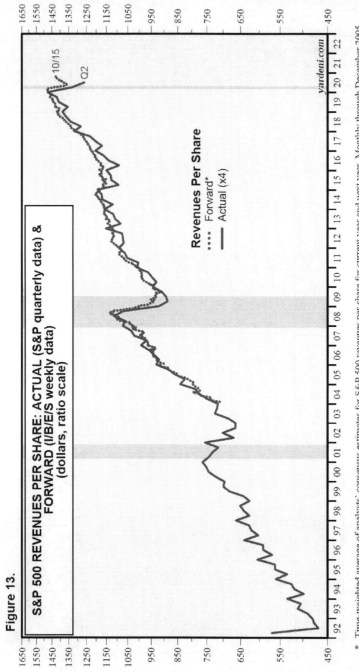

S&P 500 REVENUES PER SHARE: ACTUAL (S&P quarterly data) & FORWARD (I/B/E/S weekly data) (dollars, ratio scale)

Revenues Per Share
•••• Forward*
—— Actual (x4)

yardeni.com

* Time-weighted average of analysts' consensus estimates for S&P 500 revenues per share for current year and next year. Monthly through December 2005, then weekly.
Note: Shaded areas are recessions according to the National Bureau of Economic Research.
Source: Standard & Poor's (for actual revenues) and I/B/E/S data by Refinitiv (for forward revenues).

Figure 14.

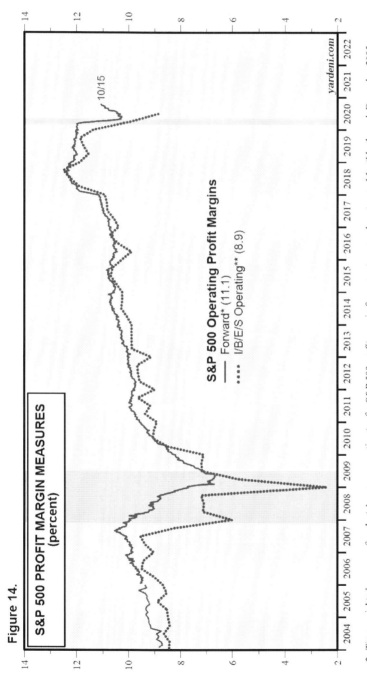

* Time-weighted average of analysts' consensus estimates for S&P 500 profit margin for current year and next year. Monthly through December 2005, then weekly.
** Operating earnings divided by revenues.
Note: Shaded areas are recessions according to the National Bureau of Economic Research.
Source: Standard & Poor's and I/B/E/S data by Refinitiv.

Figure 15.

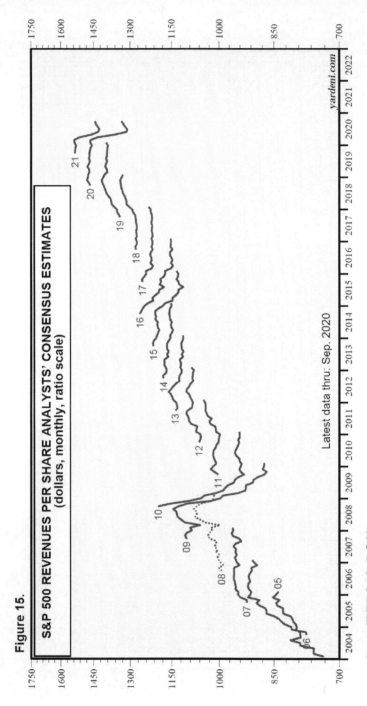

S&P 500 REVENUES PER SHARE ANALYSTS' CONSENSUS ESTIMATES
(dollars, monthly, ratio scale)

Latest data thru: Sep. 2020

Source: I/B/E/S data by Refinitiv.

Figure 16.

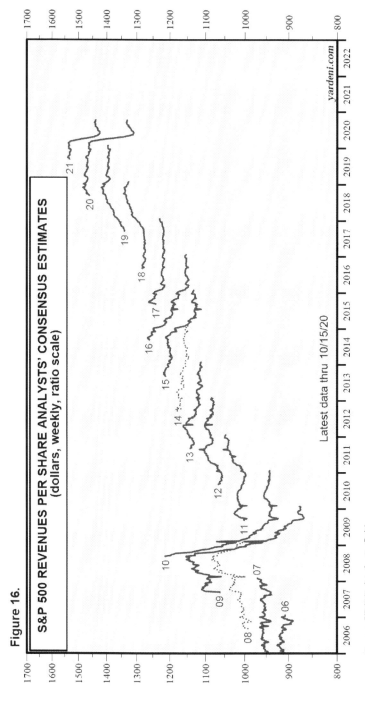

S&P 500 REVENUES PER SHARE ANALYSTS' CONSENSUS ESTIMATES
(dollars, weekly, ratio scale)

Source: I/B/E/S data by Refinitiv.

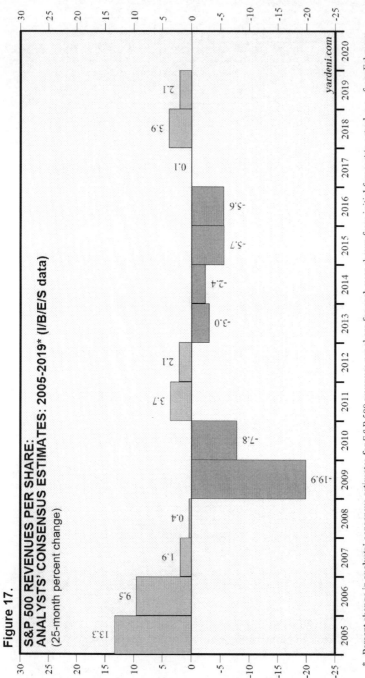

Figure 17.

S&P 500 REVENUES PER SHARE: ANALYSTS' CONSENSUS ESTIMATES: 2005-2019* (I/B/E/S data)
(25-month percent change)

yardeni.com

* Percent change in analysts' consensus estimates for S&P 500 revenues per share for each year shown from initial forecast to actual. e.g., from February 2004 to February 2006 for calendar year 2005.
Source: I/B/E/S data by Refinitiv.

Figure 18.

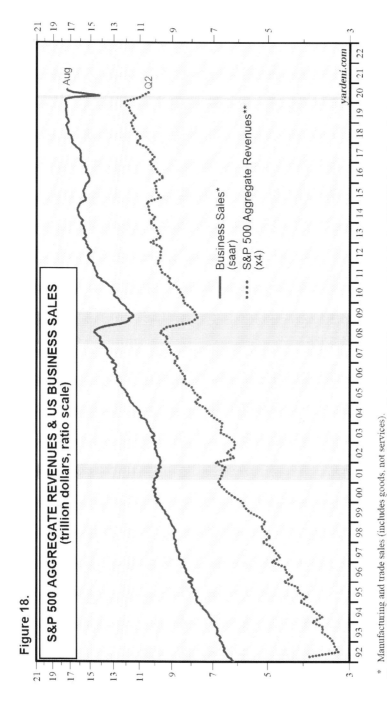

S&P 500 AGGREGATE REVENUES & US BUSINESS SALES
(trillion dollars, ratio scale)

Business Sales*
(saar)

S&P 500 Aggregate Revenues**
(x4)

yardeni.com

* Manufactuirng and trade sales (includes goods, not services).

** S&P quarterly data, not per share. Revenues are derived by multiplying S&P 500 revenues per share by the S&P 500 divisor for each quarter.
Note: Shaded areas are recessions according to the National Bureau of Economic Research.
Source: Census Bureau and Standard & Poor's.

Figure 19.

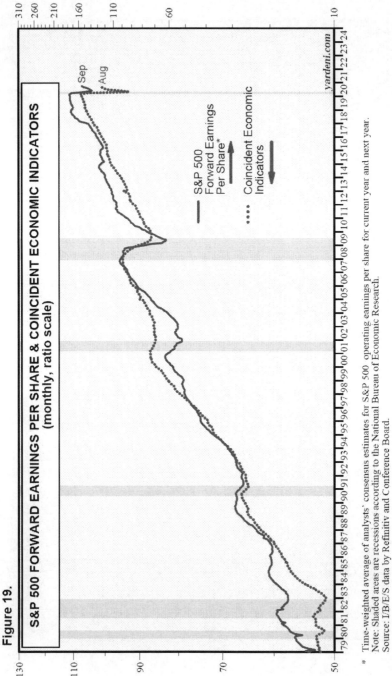

S&P 500 FORWARD EARNINGS PER SHARE & COINCIDENT ECONOMIC INDICATORS
(monthly, ratio scale)

S&P 500
Forward Earnings
Per Share*

Coincident Economic
Indicators

yardeni.com

* Time-weighted average of analysts' consensus estimates for S&P 500 operating earnings per share for current year and next year.
Note: Shaded areas are recessions according to the National Bureau of Economic Research.
Source: I/B/E/S data by Refinitiv and Conference Board.

Figure 20.

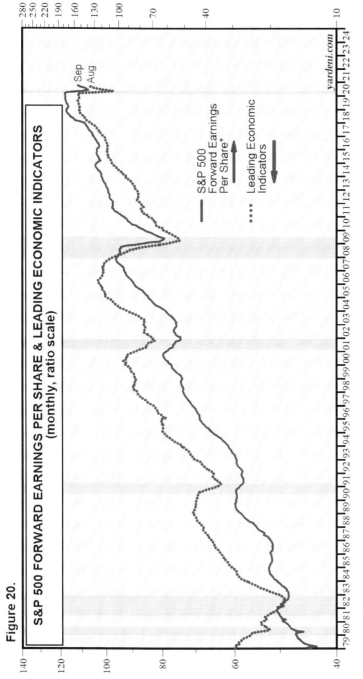

S&P 500 FORWARD EARNINGS PER SHARE & LEADING ECONOMIC INDICATORS
(monthly, ratio scale)

S&P 500
Forward Earnings
Per Share*

Leading Economic
Indicators

yardeni.com

* Time-weighted average of analysts' consensus estimates for S&P 500 operating earnings per share for current year and next year.
Note: Shaded areas are recessions according to the National Bureau of Economic Research.
Source: I/B/E/S data by Refinitiv and Conference Board.

Figure 21.

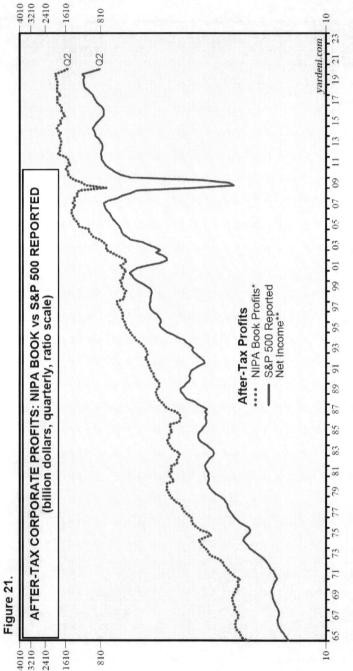

AFTER-TAX CORPORATE PROFITS: NIPA BOOK vs S&P 500 REPORTED
(billion dollars, quarterly, ratio scale)

After-Tax Profits
•••• NIPA Book Profits*
—— S&P 500 Reported
    Net Income**

yardeni.com

* NIPA book profits series excludes Inventory Valuation Adjustment and Capital Consumption Adjustment. Series is seasonally adjusted and annualized quarterly data.
** S&P 500 aggregate net income on GAAP basis using four-quarter sum.
Source: Bureau of Economic Analysis and Standard & Poor's.

Figure 22.

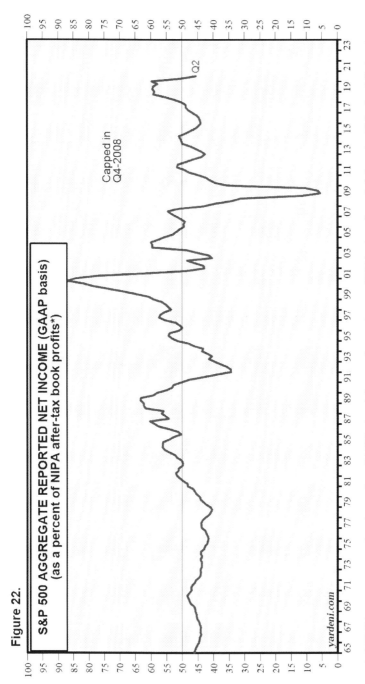

S&P 500 AGGREGATE REPORTED NET INCOME (GAAP basis)
(as a percent of NIPA after-tax book profits*)

Capped in
Q4-2008

Q2

yardeni.com

* S&P 500 aggregate reported net income is on GAAP basis and shown as four-quarter sum. NIPA book profits exclude Inventory Valuation Adjustment
and Capital Consumption Adjustment. NIPA series is shown using seasonally adjusted and annualized quarterly data.
Source: Bureau of Economic Analysis and Standard & Poor's.

Figure 23.

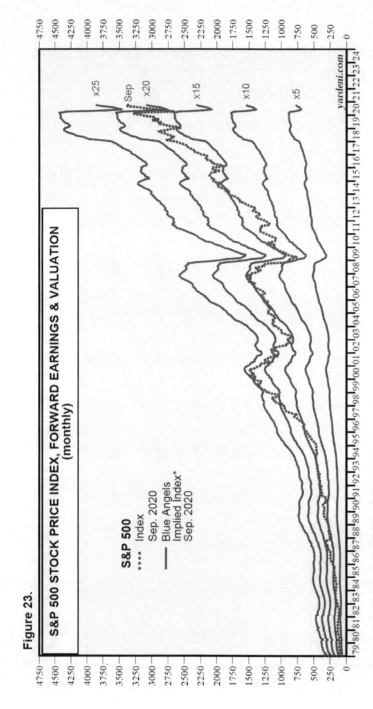

S&P 500 STOCK PRICE INDEX, FORWARD EARNINGS & VALUATION
(monthly)

S&P 500
•••• Index
    Sep. 2020
    Blue Angels
    Implied Index*
    Sep. 2020

yardeni.com

* Implied price index calculated using forward earnings times forward P/Es.
Source: Standard & Poor's and I/B/E/S data by Refinitiv.

Figure 24.

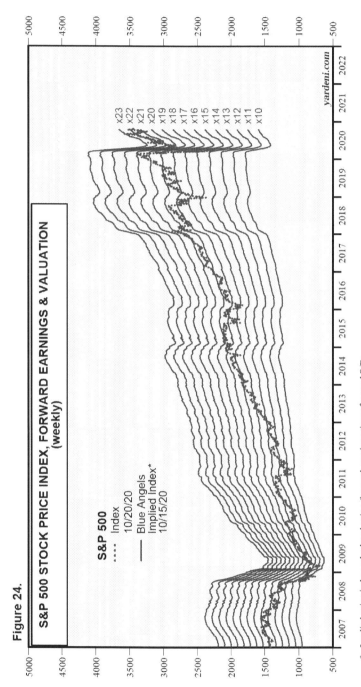

S&P 500 STOCK PRICE INDEX, FORWARD EARNINGS & VALUATION
(weekly)

S&P 500
..... Index
10/20/20
—— Blue Angels
Implied Index*
10/15/20

yardeni.com

* Implied price index calculated using forward earnings times forward P/Es.
Source: Standard & Poor's and I/B/E/S data by Refinitiv.

Figure 25.

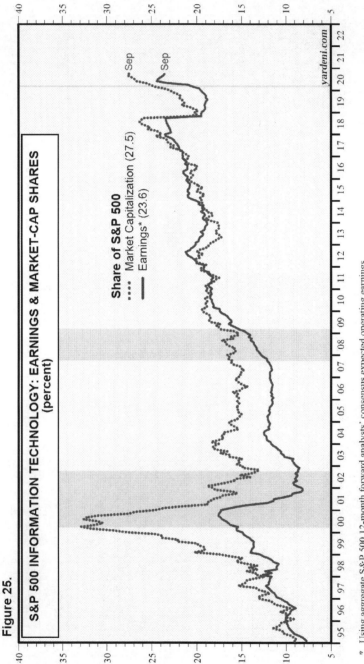

S&P 500 INFORMATION TECHNOLOGY: EARNINGS & MARKET-CAP SHARES
(percent)

Share of S&P 500
•••• Market Capitalization (27.5)
—— Earnings* (23.6)

yardeni.com

* Using aggregate S&P 500 12-month forward analysts' consensus expected operating earnings.
Note: Shaded red areas are S&P 500 bear market declines of 20% or more. Yellow areas are bull markets.
Source: I/B/E/S data by Refinitiv.

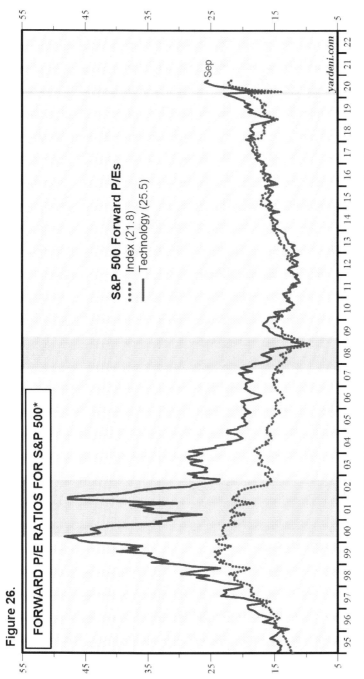

Figure 26.

FORWARD P/E RATIOS FOR S&P 500*

S&P 500 Forward P/Es
•••• Index (21.8)
——— Technology (25.5)

yardeni.com

* S&P 500 stock price index divided by S&P 500 12-month forward analysts' consensus expected operating earnings per share.
Note: Shaded red areas are S&P 500 bear market declines of 20% or more. Yellow areas are bull markets.
Source: I/B/E/S data by Refinitiv.

Figure 27.

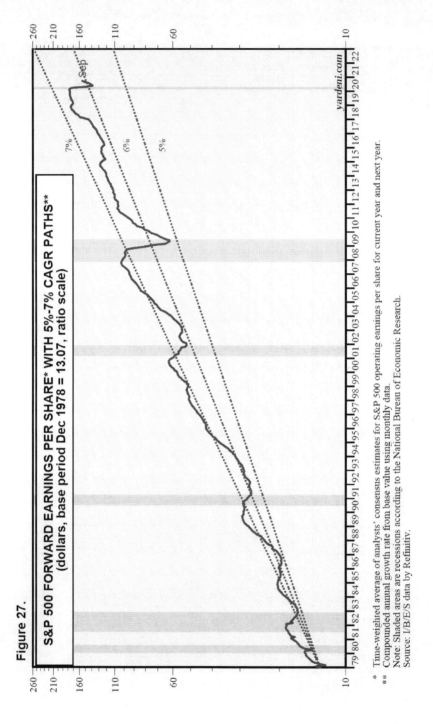

S&P 500 FORWARD EARNINGS PER SHARE* WITH 5%-7% CAGR PATHS**
(dollars, base period Dec 1978 = 13.07, ratio scale)

* Time-weighted average of analysts' consensus estimates for S&P 500 operating earnings per share for current year and next year.
** Compounded annual growth rate from base value using monthly data.
Note: Shaded areas are recessions according to the National Bureau of Economic Research.
Source: I/B/E/S data by Refinitiv.

yardeni.com

Figure 28.

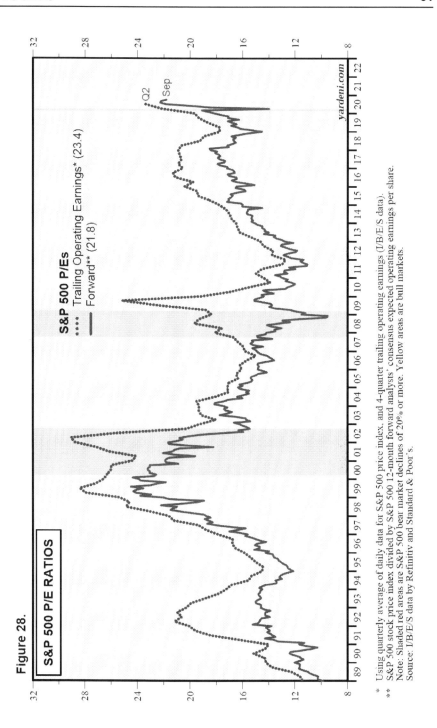

* Using quarterly average of daily data for S&P 500 price index, and 4-quarter trailing operating earnings (I/B/E/S data).
** S&P 500 stock price index divided by S&P 500 12-month forward analysts' consensus expected operating earnings per share.
   Note: Shaded red areas are S&P 500 bear market declines of 20% or more. Yellow areas are bull markets.
   Source: I/B/E/S data by Refinitiv and Standard & Poor's.

Figure 29.

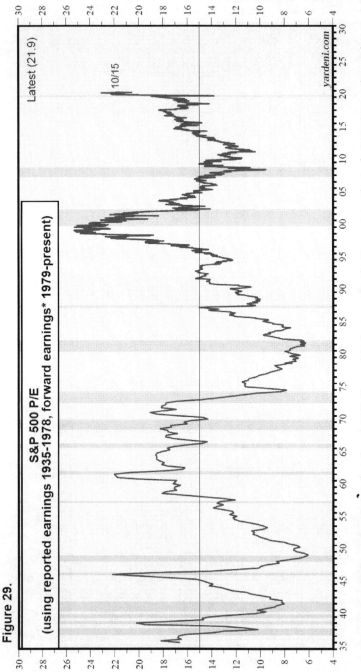

S&P 500 P/E
(using reported earnings 1935-1978, forward earnings* 1979-present)

Latest (21.9)

10/15

yardeni.com

* Four-quarter trailing sum of reported earnings through 1978. Time-weighted average of analysts' consensus estimates for S&P 500 operating earnings per share for current year and next year. Monthly from January 1979 through April 1994, then weekly.
Note: Shaded red areas are S&P 500 bear market declines of 20% or more. Yellow areas are bull markets.
Source: I/B/E/S data by Refinitiv and Standard & Poor's.

Figure 30.

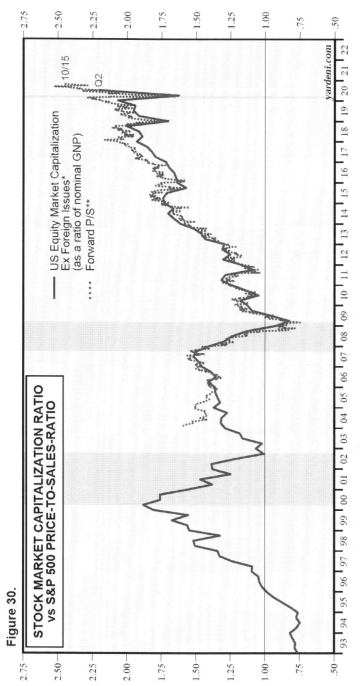

STOCK MARKET CAPITALIZATION RATIO
vs S&P 500 PRICE-TO-SALES-RATIO

— US Equity Market Capitalization
Ex Foreign Issues*
(as a ratio of nominal GNP)
···· Forward P/S**

*   Total excluding market value of holdings by US residents of foreign corporate equities, investment fund shares, and ADRs.
** S&P 500 index divided by S&P 500 year-ahead forward analysts' consensus expected revenues per share. Monthly through 2005, then weekly.
Note: Shaded red areas are S&P 500 bear market declines of 20% or more. Yellow areas are bull markets.
Source: Federal Reserve Board, Bureau of Economic Analysis, and Standard & Poor's.

yardeni.com

Figure 31.

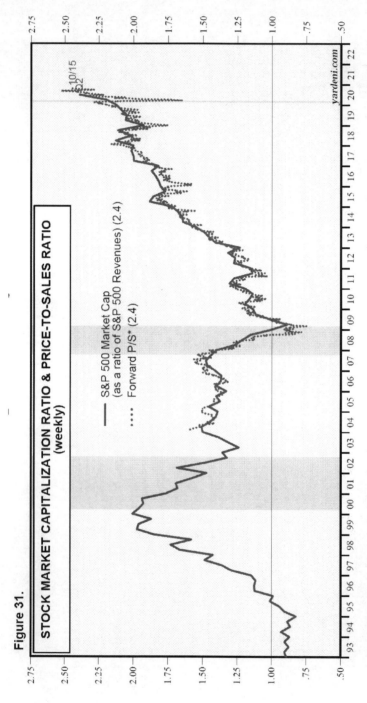

STOCK MARKET CAPITALIZATION RATIO & PRICE-TO-SALES RATIO
(weekly)

—— S&P 500 Market Cap
(as a ratio of S&P 500 Revenues) (2.4)

···· Forward P/S* (2.4)

yardeni.com

* S&P 500 index divided by year-ahead forward analysts' consensus expected S&P 500 revenues per share. Monthly through 2005, then weekly.
Note: Shaded red areas are S&P 500 bear market declines of 20% or more. Yellow areas are bull markets.
Source: I/B/E/S data by Refinitiv and Standard & Poor's.

Figure 32.

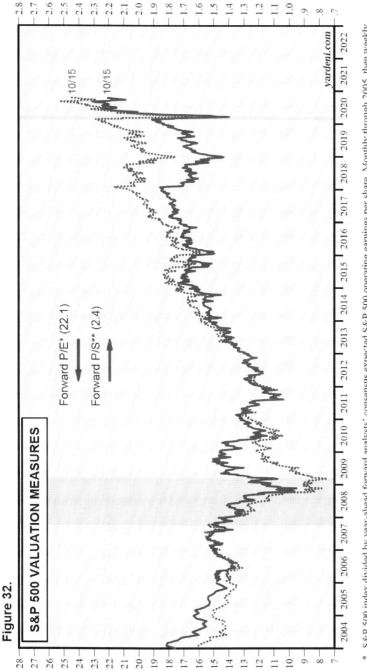

S&P 500 VALUATION MEASURES

Forward P/E* (22.1)

Forward P/S** (2.4)

yardeni.com

* S&P 500 index divided by year-ahead forward analysts' consensus expected S&P 500 operating earnings per share. Monthly through 2005, then weekly.
** S&P 500 index divided by year-ahead forward analysts' consensus expected S&P 500 revenues per share. Monthly through 2005, then weekly.
Note: Shaded red areas are S&P 500 bear market declines of 20% or more. Yellow areas are bull markets.
Source: I/B/E/S data by Refinitiv.

Figure 33.

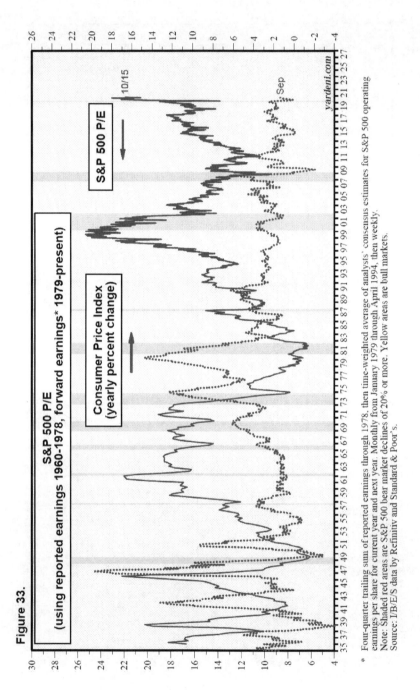

S&P 500 P/E
(using reported earnings 1960-1978, forward earnings* 1979-present)

S&P 500 P/E

Consumer Price Index
(yearly percent change)

10/15

Sep

yardeni.com

* Four-quarter trailing sum of reported earnings through 1978, then time-weighted average of analysts' consensus estimates for S&P 500 operating earnings per share for current year and next year. Monthly from January 1979 through April 1994, then weekly.
Note: Shaded red areas are S&P 500 bear market declines of 20% or more. Yellow areas are bull markets.
Source: I/B/E/S data by Refinitiv and Standard & Poor's.

Figure 34.

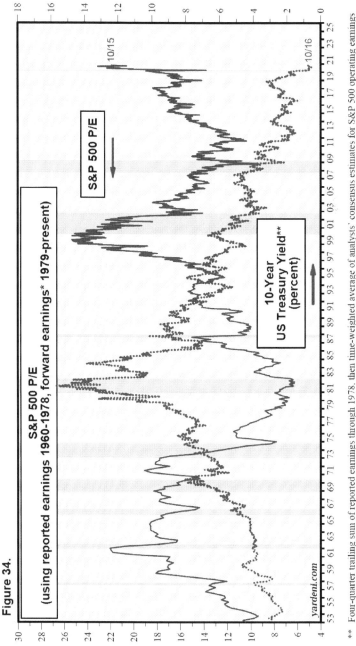

S&P 500 P/E
(using reported earnings 1960-1978, forward earnings* 1979-present)

S&P 500 P/E

10-Year
US Treasury Yield**
(percent)

yardeni.com

* Four-quarter trailing sum of reported earnings through 1978, then time-weighted average of analysts' consensus estimates for S&P 500 operating earnings per share for current year and next year. Monthly from January 1979 through April 1994, then weekly.

** Monthly from April 1953 through December 1961, then weekly.

Note: Shaded red areas are S&P 500 bear market declines of 20% or more. Yellow areas are bull markets

Source: I/B/E/S data by Refinitiv, Standard & Poor's, and Federal Reserve Board.

Figure 35.

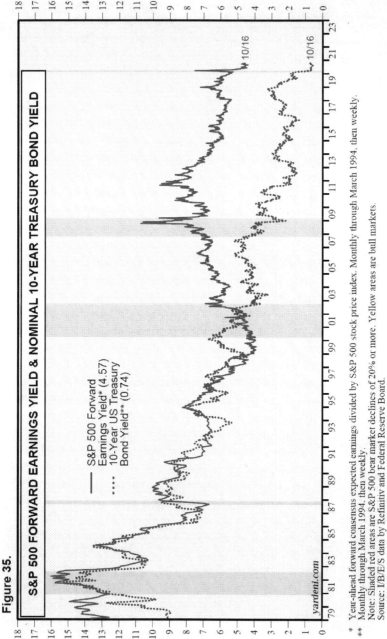

S&P 500 FORWARD EARNINGS YIELD & NOMINAL 10-YEAR TREASURY BOND YIELD

— S&P 500 Forward
    Earnings Yield* (4.57)
••• 10-Year US Treasury
    Bond Yield** (0.74)

10/16

10/16

yardeni.com

* Year-ahead forward consensus expected earnings divided by S&P 500 stock price index. Monthly through March 1994, then weekly.
** Monthly through March 1994, then weekly.
Note: Shaded red areas are S&P 500 bear market declines of 20% or more. Yellow areas are bull markets.
Source: I/B/E/S data by Refinitiv and Federal Reserve Board.

Figure 36.

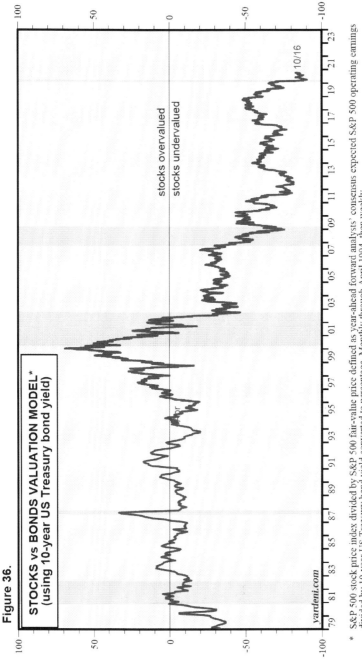

STOCKS vs BONDS VALUATION MODEL *
(using 10-year US Treasury bond yield)

stocks overvalued
stocks undervalued

10/16

yardeni.com

* S&P 500 stock price index divided by S&P 500 fair-value price defined as year-ahead forward analysts' consensus expected S&P 500 operating earnings
divided by 10-year US Treasury bond yield converted to percentage. Monthly through April 1994, then weekly.
Note: Shaded red areas are S&P 500 bear market declines of 20% or more. Yellow areas are bull markets.
Source: I/B/E/S data by Refinitiv and Federal Reserve Board.

Figure 37.

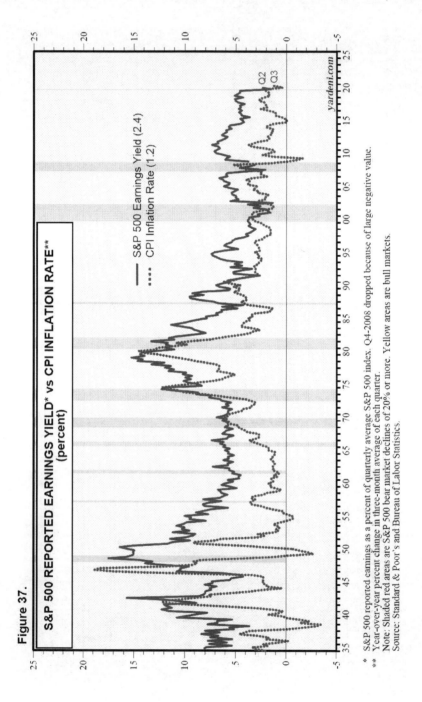

S&P 500 REPORTED EARNINGS YIELD* vs CPI INFLATION RATE**
(percent)

S&P 500 Earnings Yield (2.4)

CPI Inflation Rate (1.2)

yardeni.com

*　S&P 500 reported earnings as a percent of quarterly average S&P 500 index. Q4-2008 dropped because of large negative value.

**　Year-over-year percent change in three-month average of each quarter.

Note: Shaded red areas are S&P 500 bear market declines of 20% or more. Yellow areas are bull markets.

Source: Standard & Poor's and Bureau of Labor Statistics.

Figure 38.

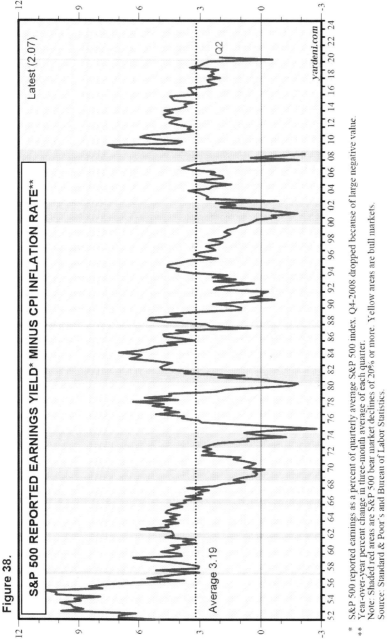

S&P 500 REPORTED EARNINGS YIELD* MINUS CPI INFLATION RATE**

Latest (2.07)

Q2

Average 3.19

yardeni.com

*   S&P 500 reported earnings as a percent of quarterly average S&P 500 index. Q4-2008 dropped because of large negative value
** Year-over-year percent change in three-month average of each quarter.
Note: Shaded red areas are S&P 500 bear market declines of 20% or more. Yellow areas are bull markets.
Source: Standard & Poor's and Bureau of Labor Statistics.

Figure 39.

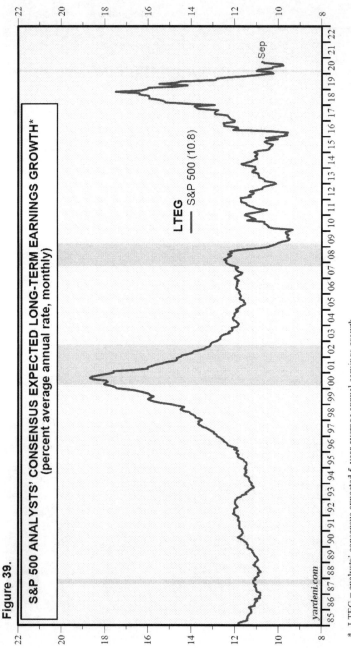

S&P 500 ANALYSTS' CONSENSUS EXPECTED LONG-TERM EARNINGS GROWTH*
(percent average annual rate, monthly)

LTEG
—— S&P 500 (10.8)

Sep

yardeni.com

* LTEG = analysts' consensus expected 5-year average annual earnings growth.
Note: Shaded red areas are S&P 500 bear market declines of 20% or more. Yellow areas are bull markets.
Source: *I/B/E/S* data by Refinitiv.

Figure 40.

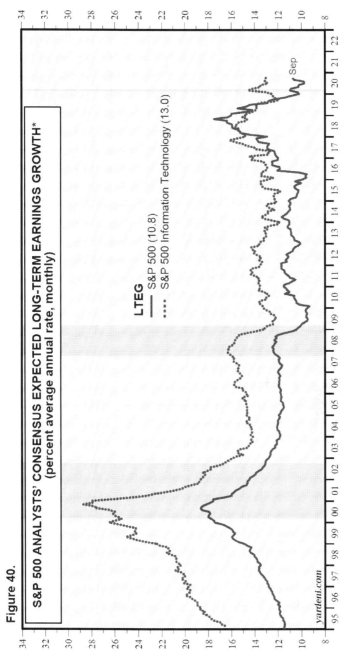

S&P 500 ANALYSTS' CONSENSUS EXPECTED LONG-TERM EARNINGS GROWTH*
(percent average annual rate, monthly)

LTEG
— S&P 500 (10.8)
····· S&P 500 Information Technology (13.0)

Sep

yardeni.com

* LTEG = analysts' consensus expected 5-year average annual earnings growth.
Note: Shaded red areas are S&P 500 bear market declines of 20% or more. Yellow areas are bull markets.
Source: I/B/E/S data by Refinitiv.

Figure 41.

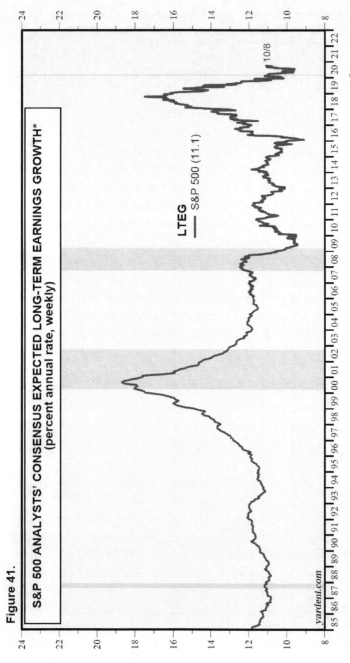

S&P 500 ANALYSTS' CONSENSUS EXPECTED LONG-TERM EARNINGS GROWTH*
(percent annual rate, weekly)

LTEG
—— S&P 500 (11.1)

yardeni.com

10/8

* LTEG = analysts' consensus expected 5-year average annual earnings growth. Monthly data through 2005, then weekly.
Note: Shaded red areas are S&P 500 bear market declines of 20% or more. Yellow areas are bull markets.
Source: I/B/E/S data by Refinitiv.

Figure 42.

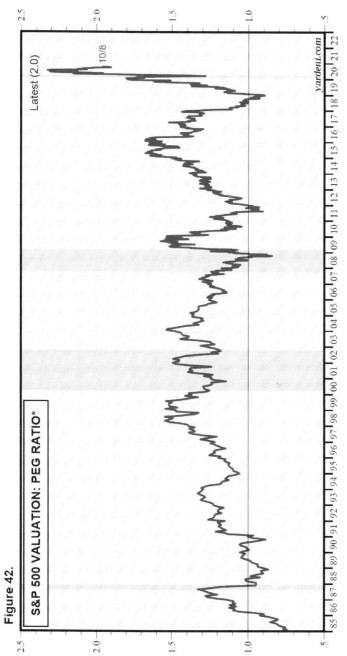

S&P 500 VALUATION: PEG RATIO*

* S&P 500 forward P/E divided by analysts' consensus expected 5-year average annual earnings growth (LTEG). Monthly data through 2005, then weekly.
Note: Shaded red areas are S&P 500 bear market declines of 20% or more. Yellow areas are bull markets.
Source: I/B/E/S data by Refinitiv.

Figure 43.

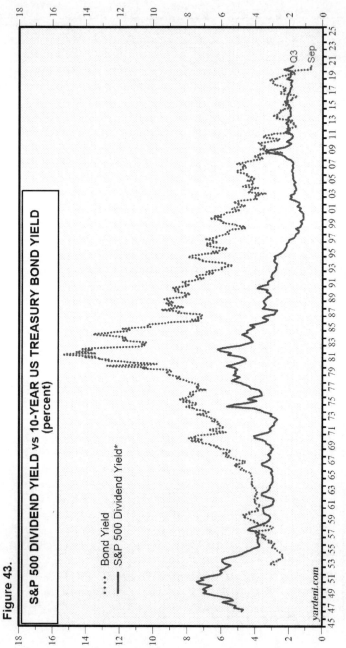

S&P 500 DIVIDEND YIELD vs 10-YEAR US TREASURY BOND YIELD
(percent)

···· Bond Yield
— S&P 500 Dividend Yield*

yardeni.com

* S&P 500 four-quarter trailing dividends per share divided by quarterly closing value of the S&P 500 index.
Source: Standard & Poor's and Federal Reserve Board.

Figure 44.

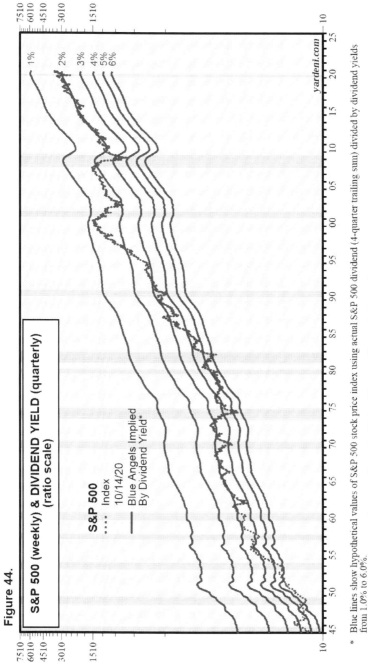

S&P 500 (weekly) & DIVIDEND YIELD (quarterly) (ratio scale)

S&P 500
  •••• Index
       10/14/20
  —— Blue Angels Implied
       By Dividend Yield*

yardeni.com

1%
2%
3%
4%
5%
6%

* Blue lines show hypothetical values of S&P 500 stock price index using actual S&P 500 dividend (4-quarter trailing sum) divided by dividend yields from 1.0% to 6.0%.
Note: Shaded areas are recessions according to the National Bureau of Economic Research.
Source: Standard & Poor's.

Figure 45.

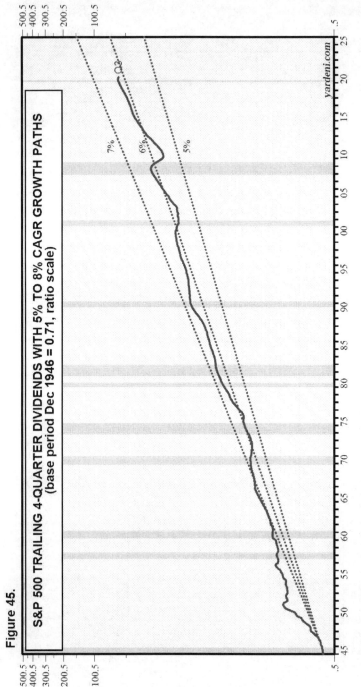

S&P 500 TRAILING 4-QUARTER DIVIDENDS WITH 5% TO 8% CAGR GROWTH PATHS
(base period Dec 1946 = 0.71, ratio scale)

Note: Shaded areas are recessions according to the National Bureau of Economic Research.
Source: Standard & Poor's.

yardeni.com

Figure 46.

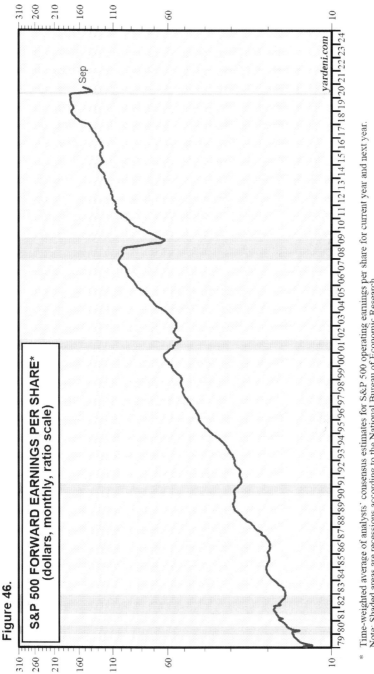

S&P 500 FORWARD EARNINGS PER SHARE*
(dollars, monthly, ratio scale)

Sep

yardeni.com

* Time-weighted average of analysts' consensus estimates for S&P 500 operating earnings per share for current year and next year.
Note: Shaded areas are recessions according to the National Bureau of Economic Research.
Source: I/B/E/S data by Refinitiv.

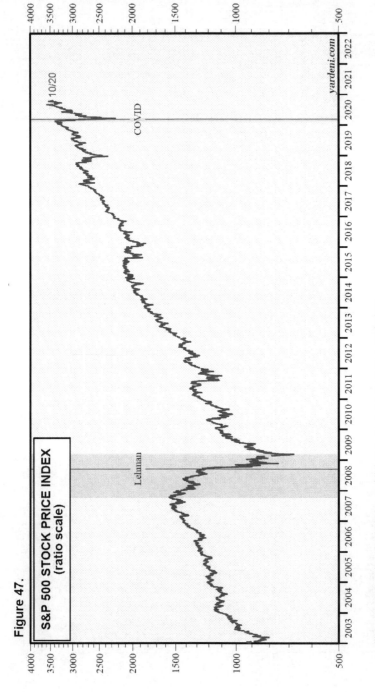

Figure 47.

S&P 500 STOCK PRICE INDEX
(ratio scale)

Note: Lehman collapsed 9/15/2008. COVID-19 declared global pandemic 3/11/2020.
Note: Shaded red areas are S&P 500 bear market declines of 20% or more. Yellow areas are bull markets.
Source: Standard & Poor's.

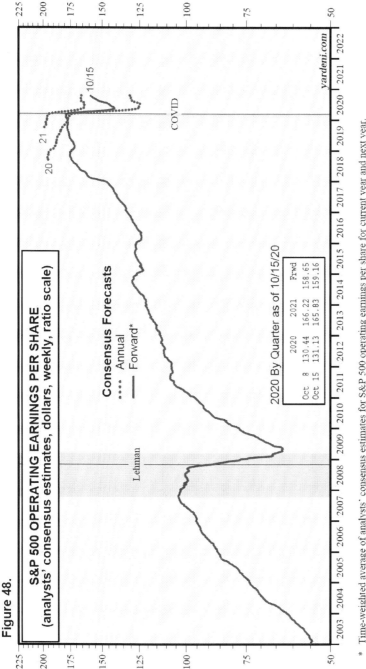

Figure 48.

S&P 500 OPERATING EARNINGS PER SHARE
(analysts' consensus estimates, dollars, weekly, ratio scale)

Consensus Forecasts
•••• Annual
—— Forward*

2020 By Quarter as of 10/15/20

	2020	2021	Frwd
Oct 8	130.44	166.22	158.65
Oct 15	131.13	165.83	159.16

Lehman

COVID

yardeni.com

* Time-weighted average of analysts' consensus estimates for S&P 500 operating earnings per share for current year and next year.
Note: Lehman collapsed 9/15/2008. COVID-19 declared global pandemic 3/11/2020.
Note: Shaded red areas are S&P 500 bear market declines of 20% or more. Yellow areas are bull markets.
Source: I/B/E/S data by Refinitiv.

Figure 49.

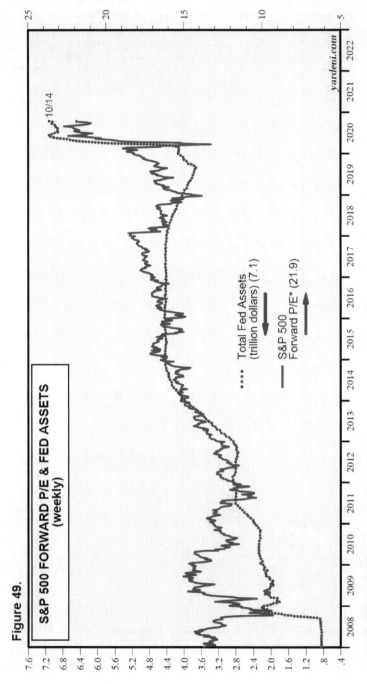

S&P 500 FORWARD P/E & FED ASSETS
(weekly)

.... Total Fed Assets
(trillion dollars) (7.1)

— S&P 500
Forward P/E* (21.9)

yardeni.com

* S&P 500 index divided by year-ahead forward analysts' consensus expected S&P 500 operating earnings per share.
Source: Federal Reserve Board. I/B/E/S data by Refinitiv. and Standard & Poor's.

Figure 50.

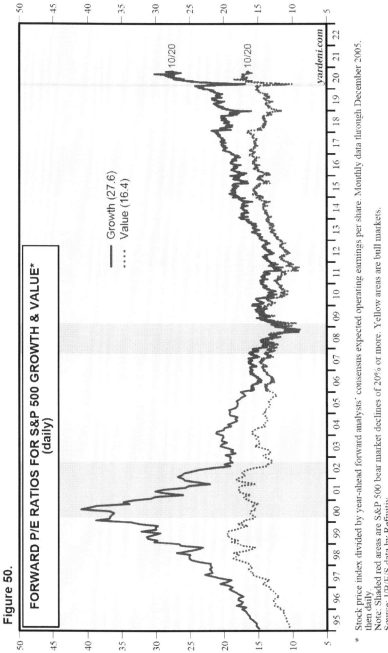

FORWARD P/E RATIOS FOR S&P 500 GROWTH & VALUE*
(daily)

—— Growth (27.6)
···· Value (16.4)

10/20

10/20

yardeni.com

* Stock price index divided by year-ahead forward analysts' consensus expected operating earnings per share. Monthly data through December 2005,
then daily.
Note: Shaded red areas are S&P 500 bear market declines of 20% or more. Yellow areas are bull markets.
Source: I/B/E/S data by Refinitiv.

Figure 51.

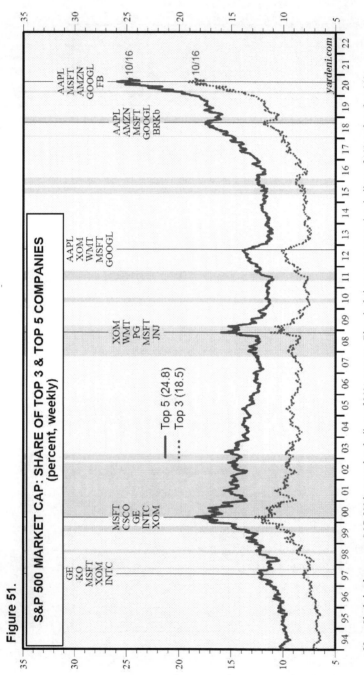

Note: Shaded red areas are S&P 500 bear market declines of 20% or more. Blue shaded areas are correction declines of 10% to less than 20%.
Yellow areas are bull markets.
Source: Yardeni Research using Standard & Poor's and I/B/E/S data by Refinitiv.

Figure 52.

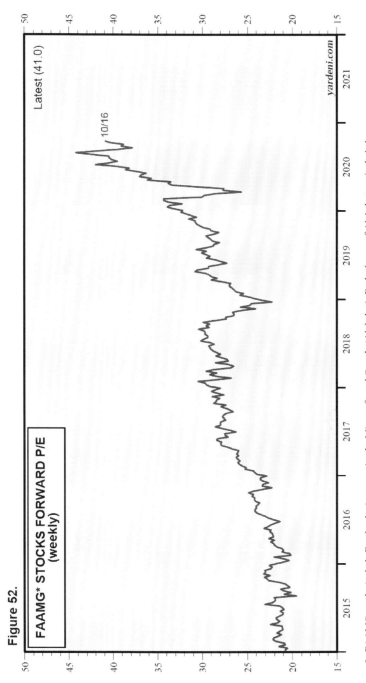

FAAMG* STOCKS FORWARD P/E
(weekly)

Latest (41.0)

10/16

*   FAAMG stocks include Facebook, Amazon, Apple, Microsoft, and Google (Alphabet). Both classes of Alphabet are included.
** Market cap divided by aggregate forward consensus expected operating earnings.
    Source: I/B/E/S data by Refinitiv.

yardeni.com

Notes

Introduction

1. See *S&P Global, S&P 500: The Gauge of the Market Economy* and *S&P U.S. Indices Methodology*, August 2020. See S&P Dow Jones Indices. spglobal.com.
2. The Global Industry Classification Standard is jointly developed and maintained by S&P Dow Jones Indices and MSCI.

Chapter 1

3. See YRI's *Stock Market Briefing: S&P 500 Earnings Squiggles Annually & Quarterly*.
4. Despite the COVID-19 pandemic, earnings during the first and second quarters of 2020 turned out to be better than the downwardly revised consensus estimates, particularly for the second quarter.
5. "NIPA Handbook: Concepts and Methods of the U.S. National Income and Product Accounts, Chapter 13: Corporate Profits," Bureau of Economic Analysis. bea.gov.
6. "Some S corporations may want to convert to C corporations," IRS. irs.gov.

Chapter 2

7. The different time series lines in our Blue Angels charts would collide if forward earnings turned negative, but this never has happened for the broad market averages we track.
8. In our January 28, 2020 *Morning Briefing*, we wrote that a P/E-led meltup increased the risk of a correction. We noted that the stock market started the year with "nothing to fear but fear itself." By the end of January, the possibility of a pandemic gave us all something to fear.
9. Alan Greenspan, "The Challenge of Central Banking in a Democratic Society," December 5, 1996 speech at the Annual Dinner and Francis Boyer Lecture of The American Enterprise Institute for Public Policy Research, Washington, D.C.
10. "Warren Buffett on the Stock Market," *Fortune*, December 10, 2001.

11. John Apruzzese, *A Reality Check for Stock Valuations,* Evercore Wealth Management, November 2017.
12. Alan Greenspan, "Rules vs. discretionary monetary policy," September 5, 1997 speech at the 15th Anniversary Conference of the Center for Economic Policy Research at Stanford University, Stanford, California.
13. Alan Greenspan, "Corporate governance," March 26, 2002 speech at the Stern School of Business, New York University, New York, New York.

Chapter 3

14. Jerome Powell, "New Economic Challenges and the Fed's Monetary Policy Review," August 27, 2020 speech at "Navigating the Decade Ahead: Implications for Monetary Policy," an economic policy symposium sponsored by the Federal Reserve Bank of Kansas City, Jackson Hole, Wyoming (via webcast).
15. Jerome Powell, July 29, 2020 Press Conference.

Made in the USA
Columbia, SC
23 November 2020